T0196602

KNOWLEDGE FOR THE SOUL

AWAKENING PEACE AND PURPOSE

BRAYDEN HALL

BALBOA.
PRESS

A DIVISION OF HAY HOUSE

Balboa Press books may be ordered through booksellers or by contacting:

Balboa Press
A Division of Hay House
1663 Liberty Drive
Bloomington, IN 47403
www.balboapress.com
1 (877) 407-4847

Because of the dynamic nature of the Internet, any web addresses or links contained in this book may have changed since publication and may no longer be valid. The views expressed in this work are solely those of the author and do not necessarily reflect the views of the publisher, and the publisher hereby disclaims any responsibility for them.

The author of this book does not dispense medical advice or prescribe the use of any technique as a form of treatment for physical, emotional, or medical problems without the advice of a physician, either directly or indirectly. The intent of the author is only to offer information of a general nature to help you in your quest for emotional and spiritual well-being. In the event you use any of the information in this book for yourself, which is your constitutional right, the author and the publisher assume no responsibility for your actions.

Any people depicted in stock imagery provided by Thinkstock are models, and such images are being used for illustrative purposes only.
Certain stock imagery © Thinkstock.

Print information available on the last page.

ISBN: 978-1-5043-2546-2 (sc)
ISBN: 978-1-5043-2548-6 (hc)
ISBN: 978-1-5043-2547-9 (e)

Library of Congress Control Number: 2014922286

Balboa Press rev. date: 09/14/2016

CONTENTS

INTRODUCTION

What if you were woken up out of oblivion and something said to you, "I have a gift for you. With this gift, you will be granted eternal awareness and have the ability to experience life"? How would you react? Each individual is being asked this question every moment. It is time to reclaim our divinity!

Finding the Meaning of Life

Who am I? Where did I come from? Why am I here? These are the greatest questions one can have on earth. Unlike most questions, we cannot find the answers through one simple Internet search. These questions inspire a lifelong journey of discovery.

When we are born, no personal manual explains the overall meaning of life and the way we are to best utilize our years. People live each day to the best of their ability, obtaining knowledge and understanding through life experiences. Based on how we have lived our lives and grown up, each person sees and relates with the world slightly different from one another and carries a variety of values, opinions, and perspectives on life.

There are so many different beliefs, debates, and discussions about why life is the way it is, as well as a wide range of practices— from science and religion to atheism and spirituality—that it can seem impossible to find all the answers about life and be confident enough to follow them.

"There must be more to life" is the basic underlying thought that pulls us toward searching for the answer to the purpose of our lives. Some people go their entire lives avoiding the question, distracting themselves instead with the contents or conflicts of the world. Other people have never thought about it because they grew up thinking this is all there is in life and never questioned it. Others have too much pride to believe in something more. But a large portion of the growing population has always been searching for the truth, reading books, going to lectures, and trying to piece together the puzzle.

The Stairway to Change

When we find our places in the world, we find it difficult to change the way we are, feel, think, and react and just what we believe in. We find ourselves continually experiencing life in our viewpoints and living with our own sets of beliefs, opinions, rules, and restrictions that have been set in our minds.

It is like we live our lives on an invisible staircase, the staircase of life. At the lower end, the steps are falling apart, cracked, and broken down. They are not very reliable. Toward the top, the condition of the steps improves and becomes more appealing. Each ascending step has a better feel to it, and you know you can trust it a little more than the one below it.

Through life experiences, we find our places on the staircase. Each of us stands on the position of the staircase we have found and come to understand, and we start to feel like it is our place on the flight of steps. It becomes normal to stay there because it is the known.

It is like we experience the world according to the position on the staircase (position in life) that we align ourselves with. Each step has a different set of rewards and limitations. With each step forward, we feel a little more clarity and freedom than we did on the previous one. The higher up the staircase of life, the more awareness and peace we experience.

When the world around us gets challenging, we often walk down a few steps. As we retreat down the staircase, our lives feel less enjoyable. We become less aware of our surroundings and more caught up in problems that arise on the lower steps (lower levels of consciousness). The farther down the staircase we go, the worse we feel about the world and ourselves.

As we experience the world, we react to it and constantly feel the need to run up and down the staircase of life. As a result, our inner feelings are always changing because we are constantly standing on different levels of the staircase and witnessing various aspects of our lives from different positions. The invisible steps of life are always stationary. We walk up and down and constantly change the way we feel.

In order to create a more enjoyable and fulfilling life experience, we need a reason to walk up the staircase and stay at the top. This book was written to inspire a foundation of knowledge that will inspire a clear path that guides us through the staircase of life so we can confidently walk the path to freedom. The reader will find excitement in the discoveries that lay ahead. Every step forward is more complete and satisfying than the one before. The higher levels of the staircase (higher levels of consciousness) are free from suffering and provide us with growing inner awareness and peace.

At the top of the staircase is the door to eternal peace, the reason why we walk up the flight of steps. Taking one step at a time, we are all united on the staircase of life, supporting each other through the journey of freedom from inner suffering.

Walking with Life

Do you ever feel like you are doing so much, yet it seems like you are getting nowhere? Every day, you wake up and dive into life where you seem to be accomplishing a lot but you feel the very same at the end of the day. It is like you know you are anxiously trying to get somewhere, but no matter what you seem to do, you find yourself in the same place. Don't worry. This is common. There is a reason we feel this way.

It is similar to when you are walking on a cruise ship in the opposite direction the boat is travelling. You sense that you are moving your legs, but you feel you aren't actually going anywhere. For example, think about walking in the opposite direction of a moving walkway in an airport or an escalator. You would have to exert continuous effort in order to move forward very slowly. The moving walkway would be travelling too fast in the opposite direction to keep up. Eventually when you got too frustrated and tired to continue moving forward, the walkway would take you right back to where you started, and you have to start all over again.

The same analogy applies to life. We can fight our way through life, keep getting frustrated and fed up with the lack of progress, and eventually burn ourselves out. Or, we can walk with life. Through knowledge, we illuminate a new life supporting path to follow.

Inspiring Happiness

We were born with a joy-filled inner child. We started our lives as innocent children with joyful sparks in the eyes. As we faced the experiences of life, we slowly became a more serious, stressed, and stubborn version of our inner child.

Just about anything amuses the inner child. When you watch a baby play with toys, you see he or she is jubilant and full of excitement. When the baby clicks a button and it makes a sound, he or she reacts as if it is the most awesome thing that has ever happened. Then he or she clicks the button again. The baby never gets tired of the joy experienced each time he or she presses the toy and it makes the sound. Ah, the good old days.

Then we become adults. Deadlines, time constraints, responsibilities, and never-ending tasks that need to be done fill our lives. We carry weights on our shoulders that feel like they are always building and nothing is ever getting removed. It feels like we are forced to do one thing after another in order to maintain our modern ways of life. This fast-paced life drowns us, making us feel unsatisfied and incomplete. Our lives become continuous automatic patterns of being temporarily satisfied and then unsatisfied. We find ourselves complacent with negative emotions, and the day of true happiness remains something that will come someday in the future.

It is time to release the weight from our shoulders and start to create our own self-sustainable happiness. Like the baby who keeps pressing the button and acts excited every time he or she hears the sound, we too can feel a consistency of excitement and joy in our lives.

Ignorance is defined as a state of being uninformed. It is a lack of understanding (lack of knowledge) and not knowing any better. Without certain knowledge and life experiences, how could people be any different than they currently are? Some people raised into this world have never been loved. How could they know any better if they don't know something better exists? Every problem stems from some sort of lack of knowledge. Human suffering results from the lack of necessary knowledge to transcend that inner suffering.

Little Johnny Just Wants Love

As you start this exciting journey, let me tell you a short story about a little boy named Johnny:

Little Johnny was born into a loving family. Love has surrounded him during his entire life, and he feels contentment and peace in his heart. He is just about to turn three years old, and his inner child is shining in all its glory. When Johnny starts school, he is introduced to a new world filled with a whole bunch of novel experiences and emotions. Little Johnny has to adapt to these new life experiences. On the first day of school, Johnny experiences a brand-new world. Class starts when the teacher asks everyone to introduce themselves. When it is Johnny's turn to tell everyone his name and age, all eyes turn to him. All of a sudden, Johnny feels an inner anxiety he has never felt before. Next, it is blocks time, a few minutes for all the kids to play with the blocks the teacher has piled on the floor. Little Johnny goes to pick up a block, Nick pushes him over, and Johnny falls to the floor. Nick laughs at Johnny and calls him a weakling. Now Johnny feels an inner fear toward something he has not felt before. When blocks time is over, Johnny has to get out crayons and paper. The teacher first shows the kids how to draw the letter A. The teacher puts the crayons on the table, and all the kids grab at them, trying to pick their favorite colors. When all the kids are done, Johnny is left with the black crayon and is filled with desire for a better color. The teacher shows everyone how to draw an A. Johnny follows her directions and makes a perfect A on his paper. He looks over at some of the other children's papers and sees his classmates scribbling random lines and shapes. Johnny feels proud he made the A. Little Megan comes up to little Johnny, steals his paper, and shows and tells everyone she drew the A. Little Johnny discovers an entirely new emotion of anger. He doesn't understand why she would do that, and he feels frustration and anger toward her. At break time, Little Johnny needs to pee. No one told him where the bathroom was in this new place. Where is it? Ah! Johnny finds a corner and pees on the floor. The teacher finds pee on the floor, and a young girl named Julia yells, "It was Johnny!" He feels humiliated, guilty, and shameful and regrets peeing on the floor where he wasn't supposed to. He goes home with all these new negative perspectives that have replaced his inner feelings of contentment. That day, Johnny went to class a loving child. He came home drowned in inner negativity, devoid of love. In just one day, he experienced a variety of negative emotions—shame, guilt, fear, desire and anger. Little Johnny realizes he felt more comfortable in the loving home and tells his mommy, "I don't want to go to school tomorrow." He feels anxiety and fear about going back. The cycle of inner suffering begins. Negative emotions become so normal by the time Johnny is an adult that he now carries them with confidence. A colder John who feels like a victim of the world replaced Little Johnny who once begged for love. John feels forced to react to the seemingly crazy, negative world with equally negative force in order to survive. The only freedom he gets is from the love of his family.

John is tired of waiting for a day to come that will bring him peace and happiness. He wants to experience it now. He searches for answers and comes across this book, which tells him that nothing in the world can change the way we feel inside without us reacting to the world and changing the way we feel toward it. It is all about our feelings and perceptions toward everything else that determines our inner feelings in each moment. Whatever thoughts and intentions we send out, we feel them. For example, loving thoughts return love. Hateful thoughts bring back anger.

John has made a new discovery. The world didn't change at all the moment he walked into his class the first day of school, where he experienced all that inner suffering. The only change was inside of him.

CHAPTER 1

AWAKENING KNOWLEDGE

Awaken knowledge to that which you already know. Realign with its truth, and open the doors to an uplifting way of relating and experiencing life.

Our True Nature

This life is about seeking to understand the deepest realities of your existence. Ask yourself questions and then pursue the answers with passion so the knowledge can be transformed into inner freedom. Doubts are replaced with understanding, which is replaced with knowingness, which transforms into inner contentment, joy, and peace.

What do we have in common with everyone else living on this planet? We are here together living through the experience of life. Each human being with free will chooses what belief system best suits him or her on his or her journey. Some believe there is a God; others refuse such an existence. Some believe there is life after death; others can't accept the fact without verifiable proof. We can accept that everyone is on his or her own path and all we can really do is focus on the direction we take in our lives.

People who are sincere about discovering the nature of their existence keep an open mind, allowing us to learn new things about the world we live in and ourselves. We can acknowledge that maybe we don't know everything and keep an open mind to learning.

Now more than ever with the material available on the Internet, one can research just about anything that piques his or her interest. A common interest is to understand more about life. Many searches each month are typed into search engines on the Internet for keywords like "What is the meaning of life?" People are wondering why we are here on earth, what's the point, and what we can do to live our lives to their greatest potential. Basically, it comes down to the question of "Who or What am I?" This is the ultimate question one can ask and, when prompted with sincerity, can lead to doorways of discovery.

When someone begins to ask the deepest questions about life, he or she can take various informative paths. A general approach of looking at all the pieces of the puzzle and then putting the pieces together for oneself is the most reinforcing route to take because it looks at all possibilities before coming to a conclusion. When this is done through simple life research, it becomes obvious that all the leading edges of discovery lead to the same path.

For example, if we look at what our ancestors were saying as far back as we can see in history, combined with the most advanced sciences in today's world, and then look at the core of religions, spirituality, and the basic underlying message in them all, we see it all leads to the same core reality. We are spiritual beings living a human experience.

After reading this, some people choose to shrug it off as meaningless. Others follow with the question, "So what does that mean?" Either way, the statement needs validation in order to be accepted as a reality.

The majority of the world has heard before that they are made of mind, body, and spirit. We know we have a mind. Else, we couldn't think. We know we have a body. Else, we couldn't move. It should be just as normal to also say we know we have a spirit. Else, we couldn't be aware. But this statement loses a lot of the population. People need proof. We can prove the mind and body. How can the spirit be proved to each and every person without a doubt? The answer is at the moment of death. The moment you pass away, the word "spirit" has never been so real. The good news is that we don't have to wait until then to understand the spirit and its meaning.

Countless books and videos available are related to near-death experiences that validate what we call "physical death" as merely a change of state of being. Nurses who work with dying patients in the hospital witness numerous occasions where patients are overstruck with awe as they experience something miraculous just before their passing.

After public speaking, the greatest fear in the world is death. Some individuals get uncomfortable talking about this and avoid the subject, but it is important to understand it for our long-term spiritual growth and know it is nothing to be afraid of. When we pass, our spirits effortlessly leave the body, where awareness remains.

We can compare death to water changing states into vapor. No one has ever died in the history of humanity; one simply changes states and lives on in another realm. It is of great relief to know that, if you live now, you will exist forever. This is not new knowledge. It has been said for thousands of years. When accepted, it can bring about a better understanding of the purpose of this life. It also helps to bring comfort to those grieving the passing of a loved one. Your special friend is safe and at peace, and you can be reunited when the time is right.

For further validation and reading, *Embraced by the Light* by Betty J. Eadie contains detailed firsthand explanations of what she experienced at the moment of leaving the body and her insights into the afterlife. This is just one-life changing story; you can discover a multitude of others by typing "near-death experience" on YouTube or a search engine.

So what does this mean? Why are we living a human experience right now when our true natures are as spiritual beings? We are here to learn. The question will be elaborated in detail to better understand what we are here to learn, what the nature of consciousness is, and what it means to exist and grow as a spirit. The material will further break down the restrictions that prevent our growth and help awaken the feeling of freedom from within to create self-sustained happiness and well-being.

Introduction to Consciousness

Consciousness means to be conscious. To be conscious means to know you exist. The term itself is defined as the state of being aware. Therefore, various degrees of consciousness can be said to be varying degrees of awareness. All living things have consciousness.

Bacteria show the beginning of the evolution process with the lowest calibrated consciousness levels on earth. As you move up the consciousness scale, you start to see insects and fish. Then as consciousness rises, predatory mammals come into play, such as lions and snakes, and we move up in expression to the bird and wolves. Finally, we reach vegetarian grazers such as the zebra, deer, pigs, monkeys, and so forth.

This information is not to be taken that humans evolve from animals, but it simply outlines everything that exists has a level of consciousness that contributes to the overall expression and experience of its reality. *Truth vs. Falsehood: How to Tell the Difference* by Dr. David R. Hawkins, MD, PhD clearly outlines the map of the scale of consciousness and detailed explanations on this subject.

A human is a conscious being and individually calibrates at a specific consciousness level based on the degree of awareness he or she is experiencing. Each individual human relates to the world a little different based on where he or she is aligned with consciousness.

Consciousness is beyond the body, feelings, and thoughts. It is beyond beliefs, attitudes, names, gender, family, and socioeconomic status. It is your core inner being and the essence of life. Consciousness is always looking to grow and expand. A very unique characteristic of a human with the mind and intelligence working in conjunction with consciousness is the ability and potential to learn to grow consciousness. Human consciousness evolves through learning. This is why it is a blessing to be born a human and elaborates on the question, "Why are we living a human experience as spiritual beings?" We are to learn to grow our inner consciousness because, after this life, the consciousness and level of awareness we have become remains.

That is, with the higher levels of consciousness, the more aware of the core reality of our existence, the more identified you are with your true nature. The more aware we are of our core reality, the better the experience becomes. So, the goal of earthly life is to clearly raise levels of awareness to ultimately find our true natures so we can experience that cognizance when we leave the body.

Spiritual University on Earth

We can see the world as a spiritual university or playground. We chose to come to earth and learn. This truth puts a very different perspective on life. Living as the victim of life means we are wasting our own time. It is like you really wanted to be a star player on the national football team, and when granted your wish to be a player, instead of embracing the opportunity, you decided to sit on the ground with your arms crossed, refusing to have fun playing. We wanted to be here and experience the happenings of our lives for our own karmic and spiritual growth. It is our responsibility to live this truth for its own sake. We don't point fingers in the game of life.

The way we choose to live our lives now that we are here determines if we are using this life for the benefit of our spiritual growth.

On earth, we are separated from one another with the appearance of individuality. It is purposely set up this way so each and every person is responsible for his or her own choices coming from within him or her. Blessed with the power of free will and choice, we choose how we live, act, and react to the world and what we feel toward others. This is why carnation into this world is the quickest avenue for spiritual growth. Here on earth, we have complete free will to create our own destinies. What better place to grow where we actually have free will to choose between "positive" and "negative" in each instance. Based on our intention toward all aspects of life determine if one is expanding his or her consciousness or limiting growth. Expanding one's consciousness is the process of becoming more like the source. The source of life is the highest consciousness possible.

Learning to Love

A commonality arises in each one of the near-death experiences that tells us something very important about life. An overwhelming sense of unconditional love and joy is present in the realms of heaven. Each person who has travelled to the afterlife and reconnected with the source of existence says, "There is nothing but unconditional love, joy, and peace."

This gives us very useful knowledge that we can use for our own inner growth. All the negative judgmental versions and depictions of what people see God as can be surrendered as falsehood. God, as the source, is incapable of judgment. Only humans do that.

The term "unconditional" means unwavering and absolute. So to believe in God is to believe in unconditional love, not some man sitting in a chair eating pretzels while judging the acts of his creations and punishing them for wrongdoings. This knowledge that God is unconditional, all-encompassing, joyous love paints a very different picture about the purpose of our individual lives. God is the source of all life, and love is our true nature.

The purpose of life on earth is to therefore to learn how to love unconditionally. When we do so, consciousness finds its way back to source energy. In other words, here on earth, we are on the path to become unconditionally loving beings.

Negativity and judging toward others and ourselves can be relinquished for it has no purpose and takes us away from reality. Instead, we exhibit love for all we can and ourselves. All love we exhibit here comes back to us in this life and for eternity.

What Is Love

Love is the infinite governing power. This energy stems from creation and sustains all life. If there were no love, there would be chaos, and life would destroy itself. Just using one simple example, if a mother did not love her children, she would abandon them. Without love, there is war and disaster. With love, there is unity and harmony.

The term "love" appears throughout this book, so we should start with a clear explanation of what kind of love we are discussing. The love talked about in this book is not a relationship love per se. It is more of a lighthearted way of being in the world. You could call it a spiritual or compassionate love.

Spiritual love is an inner love that radiates from within us to all of life. It is a way of expanding love to the world so the joyous experience can be maintained at all times. Its effects are uplifting, healing, fulfilling, and self-rewarding and filled with compassion and forgiveness. This type of love is not an emotional love or affection toward something. Emotional love is based on the misconception that something has to be "mine" in order to for us love it. She is my wife, so I love her. That is my dog, so I love it.

Spiritual love is not restricted to a relationship or set under conditions. Spiritual love is a way of expressing oneself in the world, and it is not selective. All encompassing, it isn't taken away if conditions aren't favorable. We release love for the sake of spreading positive and healing energy.

The payoff to lovingness is self-rewarding and fulfilling. When we radiate love, we feel a positive change in our inner experience.

> Most humans believe that love is something that you get, that it is an emotion, that it has to be deserved, and that the more they give away, the less they will have. The opposite is the truth. Lovingness is an attitude that transforms one's experience of the world. We become grateful for what we have instead of prideful. We express our lovingness when we acknowledge others and their contributions to life and to our convenience. Love is not an emotion but a way of being and relating to the world. Love is misunderstood

to be an emotion; actually it is a state of awareness, a way of being in the world, a way of seeing oneself and others. Love for God or nature or even one's pets open the doors to spiritual inspiration. The desire to make others happy overrides selfishness. The more we give love, the greater our capacity to do so becomes. It is a good beginning practice to merely mentally wish others well throughout the course of the day. Love blossoms into lovingness, which becomes progressively more intense, nonselective and joyful. (Hawkins 2011, 120)

This information gives us a new outlook on what real love is. If our purpose is to learn love, we can use this lifetime as a stepping stone to speed up the process and once again be reunited with the energy that sustains life.

God

A false depicted version of God is spread through the world. The term itself has been so misleading that when someone thinks of God, he or she may fear being judged for past actions. This is maybe why the Buddha did not use the word in his teachings. This fear-based version of God is a major hindrance to one's spiritual growth. It is falsehood and should be treated as such. Because the word *God* has been so abused, other terms are beneficial to use to describe the same universal energy, such as Allness, Oneness, Source, Creation, Holy Spirit, Divinity, or even just Life.

So what is God anyway? God is infinite love. To believe in love is to believe in God. All great things are simple. Divinity is the all-loving energy of creation. It is the underlying source of existence that is the unconditional love that gifts the freedom to be breathe, experience, exist, and be aware that we are cognizant.

Without Divinity, there would be oblivion—no awareness, no life source, and no love. With Divinity, there is beautiful life and the ability to experience, be alive, and feel love and joy.

The very core of all existence is Divinity, and it is the same in all of us, the light of love, the gift of life, and the everlasting moment of awareness that is experienced. The source of life is the highest reality of consciousness and always expanding its consciousness at the speed of light. This is why we have life. We are units of consciousness, learning and evolving to find our way back "home" to reconnect with source. The journey to God is like a reader wanting to meet the author or a person watching a movie and wanting to meet the producer. It is just that. You come to appreciate and respect life to the extent you seek to live with the energy that created life by becoming one with its nature.

God is not something out there that is separate from you. To exist is to be in the presence of God. All forms of existence therefore carry the presence of God within. God is eternal within the spirit—always present, always aware, and always loving. To awaken its presence, we align with its love. We become channels of God's unconditional love.

The core essence of God is formless. When we put structure on God, it creates limitations, but its infinite energy has no restrictions. Any term used to describe "God" itself can be surrendered because that which it truly is has no label. But let's not get too technical. All we really need to acknowledge is God as source is infinite love, joy and peace.

We can let go of the illusion of being separate from God that restricts the experience of its glory. God is not somewhere up in the sky. It is within you. Love the created as the creator.

Spiritual Path

All creation comes from the same source. Nothing that exists can create itself. Did you create yourself? This means a life source exists that is far greater than our understanding.

A human being is the physical form of a spiritual being. The spirit is a child of the Holy Spirit. Within all spirits is the potential to experience the Holy Spirit in all of its glory. The creator resides in all of its creations. It is like the Holy Spirit is the sun and the rays of lights shining from the sun are the spirits. All spiritual beings carry the light of the creator within, and this one source connects all spirits. Spiritual work is therefore a pathway to realize one's full potential as source. Lead by the divinity of the light. The spirit can find its way back home.

Spirituality is a lifelong journey that involves going from the viewpoint of ordinary to extraordinary, making the impossible possible, feeling incomplete to complete, changing thinkingness into lovingness, and transforming identification from the physical to the nonphysical, and moving beyond the visible and developing a faith in relying on the nonvisible energy that sustains life. To be spiritual means you want to go beyond basic survival and pursue a deeper understanding of life and what it means to exist.

Something inside everyone knows there is life beyond physicality. Else, what is the purpose of looking for life guidance, seeking knowledge, and searching for answers to your deepest questions? If life were just a temporary experience, than why would people be wasting their time learning when they only have a limited time to live and experience?

The quality inside everyone that is searching for truth is the inner spirit or soul, which intrinsically knows there is life beyond the physical and seeks knowledge to utilize the time he or she has on earth to maximize its potential to grow so this lifetime is a worthwhile venture. The growth that is obtained here is carried for eternity. That is why knowledge is freedom.

For the serious spiritual seeker, he or she focuses on the deepest core of his or her existence and searches for the way to awaken it as the primary experience. He or she realizes this is the most precious thing one can do in life.

Magnificent Being

A magnificent being, filled with great power, is inside of you. To experience this inner being, one must live in harmony with it. Once awakened, the spirit is free to express its divine potential. The liberating experience of the magnificent being is the same in all humans because it is connected to the source of life. When the powers of the source are summoned, ordinary becomes extraordinary. How do you know if you are living with your magnificent being? Ask yourself, "Am I editing the perfection of life? Or am I living in harmony with it?"

Characteristics of the *magnificent being* include love-filled, complete, peaceful, joyful, lighthearted, accepting, powerful, positive, lovable, unconditional, patient, helpful, nonjudgmental, encouraging, inspirational, beautiful, compassionate, forgiving, innocent, integrous, humble, humorous, thankful, vibrant, alive, happy, aware, safe, relaxed, comfortable, fearless, and fulfilled.

Identifying and aligning oneself with these characteristics brings you closer to your true nature of being. When you find yourself experiencing something other than these, see it as an indicator that you are not aligned with your core reality. The more out of touch, the more suffering is experienced because it requires tiresome energy to fight back with how nature intended to express itself. Great relief comes when we stop using our energies to deny our inner greatness. We can then use the energy to tap into the inner magnificent being waiting to express itself. When negativity ceases, joy arises. The more harmonious we live with life, the more fulfilling the life experience becomes.

So what does it mean by editing the perfection of your magnificent being?

- judging, condemning, or criticizing
- thinking negatively toward oneself or others
- seeking revenge, gain, and control and power
- exhibiting anger and hatred
- fearing
- having never-ending desire
- wanting to be right or feel better than or special
- feeling like the victim
- being unforgiving or not compassionate
- not caring for yourself or others
- not loving or accepting
- being attracted to chaos
- having negative reactions
- forcing
- having unsatisfied behavior
- being impatient, rude/ignorant, or arrogant
- dwelling on negativity

Purpose of Human Life

This writing provides information to grow one's inner happiness by developing a better understanding of life. Of course, everyone has different opinions and perspectives about life and the purpose of our years on earth that relate specifically to him or her. This section briefly describes the overall generic purpose of human life from a spiritual perspective.

Jesus Christ said, "In my father's house are many mansions." (John 14:2, King James Bible). From this quote, we can take that life after earth has many stages from astral, purgatorial, limbo, and celestial realms of heaven. Each spirit rises to the level of consciousness that has been attained on earth by what he or she has become. Depending on the consciousness (level of awareness of reality) of the individual has a direct influence on the afterlife. Have no fear. We have been there before, and different degrees of peacefulness are present in almost all levels of the evolutionary process. The consciousness level of love is of the heavenly celestial realms and everyone's ultimate destiny.

We can look at earth as home away from home, a vacation from our natural state, if you will. We took the vacation to grow our inner wisdom and knowledge to advance into higher realms of existence. It is like a vacation of schooling to grow so that, when we get back home, we can literally experience the knowledge we picked up on earth. When we learn to love on earth, we can experience that love for eternity back home.

The general purpose of life is to learn to become one with our inner magnificent beings and identify with its liberating qualities.

Snowflake Analogy

We can see life like a snowy windstorm in which each human being is like a single snowflake floating through the sky. Every snowflake is unique and perfect and equally important in its role in becoming snow. As the snowflakes travel through the sky, nonvisible wind tunnels take snowflakes in various directions. The snowflakes (like humans) go from one wind tunnel to another (one inner feeling to another) and take routes off the straight and narrow path of its ultimate destiny.

Eventually, the snowflake chooses not to attach to any of the wind tunnels and simply let itself gracefully fall (surrender, stop resisting, and attaching to negative emotions) where it is destined to go. The snowflake (human being) is free from the wind (inner suffering) and aligned with its ultimate destiny, to fulfill its purpose and become one with the snow (one with love).

From This Moment On

From this moment on,
change the way you see yourself.
Think of yourself as a spirit,
a divine energy created by God.
Identify with this inner spirit,
and gain strength from its peaceful nature.
Focus your attention on the growth of this spirit,
and learn how to fill it with love.

The world is the way it is for this very reason.
Life experiences are opportunities.
Understanding and acceptance are the keys to freedom.
Compassion lets us see the innocent spirit in others.
It is easier to forgive and release our love and feel safe doing so.
We become increasingly aware of the miracle of life.
Thankfulness builds a foundation for inner power to grow.
Joy is carried within,
and lovingness becomes the commonplace.

Reawakening Reality

Every instance, every moment, every second is an unfolding and revealing of the miracle of life. Life is a never-ending gift that keeps on being given. Because the miracle is so consistent and unwavering, in the eyes of the average human, it is considered normal or just another moment. Life and existing itself is the biggest thing taken for granted. Life is kind of seen like, "Yeah? So now what?" So the pursuit for something more, better, and more satisfying prevails. Apparently to the average person, existing just isn't good enough. The sad truth is that some people are less excited about their actual life than getting something like a new car or lump sum of money. Since childhood, we have been programmed that this life is all about getting and acquiring that we sometimes don't even take a second and look at what we have, life!

To find freedom from the never-ending pursuit of desire, stay consciously aware of the reality of the miracle of living and greatness of each very instance. We realign ourselves with the gift of experiencing. Isn't it amazing to simply be something at all?

We as a human race have gone so far outside of ourselves in an effort to make our lives perfect that we have become like the ball in a pinball machine constantly being tossed around, thrown into this feeling to that. The problem lies in our identification. We have been associating ourselves solely with the ball in the pinball machine and ignoring the magnificence of the entire creation. In other words, we have been identifying solely on the content of our minds, physical possessions, social status, and the external activities happening in our lives that we have ignored the greater life energy that we are.

The best part about life is that we are here in the first place experiencing, isn't it? If you are looking for a sense of peace, identify with the feeling of life within you, which is already at peace. You do not need to look for something amazing that will fall out of the sky one day. We already carry the complete package within us. Everything else beyond the simplicity and perfection of existing is just a bonus, more gifts from creation that we can be thankful for.

Before we were alive, out of oblivion, if someone would have suddenly described what existing, being something, or feeling alive meant and all that comes with it, we would be thrilled about being involved in such a thing. The response would be something like, "You mean you are going to give me life, and I'm only asked to have a good time and be happy, joyful, and full of love? Okay! Pick me! Pick me! I want to do it!"

So now we are here. Why are we having such a difficult time? What has turned the miracle into a hassle, stress, and form of suffering? In reality, we only had a few things on our lives' to-do lists. Suffering in the form of inner negative emotions was not on the register. Inner suffering is never justified. It is the opposite of what we are to do as a unit of creation. Suffering is only part of the learning process so we can rise above it and find joy.

We can compare life to opening a fresh can of the most beautiful and vibrant rainbow color paint. Instead of using it to paint our pictures, we drop dabs of black paint (negative emotions), mix it around into the concoction, and use this to paint instead. Then we wonder why our paintings (our lives) don't look perfect and isn't turning out how we expected.

In other words, we shouldn't cover the beauty of what life gave us with negative emotions. If you want to live the good life, paint your life with the magnificence you were given and try not to allow any spots of darkness to be added to the internal mixture.

It is time to show life why it created us by living with love, purpose, and passion. We are living and breathing right now to fulfill our potentials and have fun through the process. Let us rediscover the joy of being alive and through knowledge break down the restrictions that prevent us from experiencing that joy always.

CHAPTER 2

THE MIND

This section gives us a better understanding of the human mind. This is a crucial part of the process to creating inner contentment because it describes the causes of inner suffering.

Learning the Mind

The human mind, what a blessing and what a curse. What a blessing it is to have a mind capable of having awareness, learning, solving problems, creating, communicating, and doing everything else that is only possible because of the mind. With this mind comes a dilemma, a never-ending struggle between truth and falsehood and positive and negative. The mind is a powerful tool. When it focuses on the positive, an affirmative inner experience prevails. But when it focuses on negativity, the mind can become a form of despair and relentless suffering. So why are we so susceptible to negativity and suffering in the mind?

From the day we are born, we are instilled with individual belief systems. These belief systems are shaped through the way we were raised, our parents' values, living environment, life experiences, and so forth. We protect our principles with all seriousness when we feel they are being threatened even if the very belief system is not aligned with making us feel good.

Where did a belief system come from in the first place? Where did all of them come from? The mind heard something somewhere by someone it trusted, picked it up, and then recorded it as knowledge worth holding onto. Later, the mind will then relay what it heard and claim it as its own belief. There is nothing wrong with believing in anything, but too many people have false-based belief systems that are not aligned with their overall well-being. What to believe has been so engrained into us that it is sometimes even too hard to see that what we claim to believe in is only causing inner stress and promoting unsatisfied behavior.

Think back to when we were children. The innocence of a child's mind is such that you can tell him or her just about anything and he or she will believe you. That child is still in us, waiting for someone to tell us what is right and wrong and show us the way. As adults, that child is hidden underneath multiple layers of belief systems that have been established through years of life experiences. As we grow older, we continue to obtain knowledge until we are confident and comfortable with our views on life.

Our minds constantly record the world, storing details into different categories and revolving everything around us. In our experiences of life, we are the central character. As we witness each moment of existence, the mind picks up on incoming stimuli, and then we react at astonishing speeds with thoughts and emotions that seem appropriate to us. The human mind works to record that which is experienced and organize everything into categories of importance. Depending on how important we see something to be, it will determine if it provides us with gratification. For example, if we see money as important, we feel good when we get it.

The main goal of the mind is to maintain survival. The mind thinks it will only be something and be able to continue to survive if it edits that which is witnessed and creates a separate view and reaction to it. These reactions determine our feelings. When it seems appropriate to the mind, the reaction will be positive or negative.

The mind thinks it is separate from everything else, so it feels the need to react to everything accordingly. Through our reactions, which are based on the thoughts in our minds, we literally create the world we feel and experience. This discovery is necessary to for us to begin the process of changing the way we feel inside.

First, the mind's first interest is solely survival, not happiness. Even when the mind has negative thoughts and feelings toward something that doesn't make us feel good, it will still claim there is a good reason why we should be focusing on it in that moment. The mind has no problem feeling negative emotions because its primary motive is survival and protecting itself, not feelings. It operates under conditions. According to the mind, happiness comes only when the right circumstances are met. For example, it thinks, "If this expectation and requirement are met, then I will be happy."

The human mind is set up to constantly change its view of life according to the happenings of the external world. When things go our way, the mind tells us that life is good. When things start to waver from how we planned, expected, or wanted, the mind tells us life has become less fulfilling, and we end up feeling like the victim of the experience for one reason or another which results in feeling inner suffering.

As humans, our minds can experience a wide range of emotions that range from the following negative to positive experiences:

Negative

- humiliation (shame)
- blame (guilt)

- despair (apathy)
- regret (grief)
- anxiety (fear)
- craving (desire)
- hate (anger)
- scorn (pride)

Positive

- affirmation (courage)
- trust (neutrality)
- optimism (willingness)
- forgiveness (acceptance)
- understanding (reason)
- reverence (love)
- serenity (joy)
- bliss (peace)

The list above was outlined using the map of scale of consciousness found in *Power vs. Force* (Hawkins 1995).

When we recognize these feelings in our lives, we can see how different aspects of our lives can be organized under various emotional categories. In the table above, the text in parentheses shows the feeling that results from reaction/intention we send out. The responses we send out are based on our minds telling us it is appropriate to attach to certain thoughts and feelings under specific circumstances. We can react to something with humiliation and feel shame based on that response. We can react to something with forgiveness and feel acceptance. When we react with hate, we feel anger. When we react with reverence, we feel love. We create our inner feelings toward life according to our various reactions and inner intention.

It seems as though we are victims of our minds, made to feel certain ways about specific situations because the mind tells us it is appropriate at that time. Our thoughts constantly race and take us into different worlds, and we feel the resulting emotional feelings based on the thoughts to which we attach and identify with. The negative thoughts we identify with cause suffering.

To be free from all inner suffering experienced within the mind, surrender the energy we have been giving our negative reactions. With awareness to what is going on in our minds, we can decide our reactions, which determine our feelings.

Understanding the Ego (False Self)

There is much more to human beings than can be seen on the surface. Why are some people happy and others sad or angry all the time? What makes everyone different? How can people have completely dissimilar experiences during the same events? What makes each one of us act in his or her own unique way? What makes us feel separate?

It is the thing inside our minds called the "ego," which is the ultimate "me." The term is quite well known and commonly referred to when someone says, "Oh, that person has a big ego." The ego, or the "false self," is an animal-driven quality that is active to different degrees in all human minds until the state of enlightenment. The ego was established into the physical makeup in order to maintain survival as consciousness progressed. In the early history of humans, the ego's automatic reactions were necessary to determine friend from enemy, find food, and maintain survival. If we think about it, if there were no ego, humans would not have had any driving force to stay alive.

Now with our advanced and modern ways of living, the ego is not necessary and does more harm than good. The ego's automatic reactions cause us to feel shame, guilt, apathy, grief, fear, desire, and anger in the form of suffering. Without the ego, we would not experience any of these feelings. All of these feelings are simply triggers that use to provide a sense of self-guidance and protection. Now, they only cause pain and suffering.

The ego wants to be the best, richest, fastest, strongest, most likeable, smartest, popular/famous, best looking, and so forth. The ego wants to be in the spotlight, have the most material things, always win and feel worse when it loses, control everything and expect everything to be in its best interest, feel special and better than others, and so on. Because of these never-ending wants and the inability for us to satisfy them all, we experience forms of suffering.

Instead of denying that we have an ego, it is beneficial for us to laugh at it and realize that everyone has it. It is good to say to our egos, "Of course you want to be the best looking" ... "Of course you want to win" ... "Of course you wish they hadn't said that" ... "Of course you want to be famous." You simply see the long list of wants the ego sends you. The ego's wants never end. That is why, when some people get rich and are identifying to a large degree with the ego mind, they adapt a new want and find it hard to experience that moment of true inner happiness.

The false self as ego tries and usually succeeds at controlling the instant reaction in our minds. When someone says something negative to us, we sometimes almost instantly feel anger toward that person because the ego feels threatened and needs a justifiable reaction. The bigger our reactions toward the world, the more power our egos have to use against us. When we have big negative reactions, the ego believes it is in danger and goes into survival mode that triggers certain feelings in order to protect its own identity and make it know how to act next. The problem is the more the ego and its reactions are dominating, the less the lighthearted, joyful spirit can shine through.

There is no use getting mad at the ego because it is innocent in its design. It bases everything in terms of survival and nothing else. When humans feel a negative emotion, such as anger toward anything, the ego is merely doing what it intrinsically knows, so that consciousness could survive. So while we are getting angry about something like someone cutting us off in traffic—which is no threat to our survival—the ego interprets the anger as if it were in danger and responds with the inner feeling to protect its existence. Human beings have accepted the ego's natural responses into our daily lives, and now it feels more normal than not.

As we go through life from one experience to the next, the ego finds ways to sneak into our consciousness, attach on to negative thinking, and make us feel the resulting inner suffering. In one day, we can go from being satisfied when we wake up and drink our coffees to being sad about the cut in bonuses at work, angry that the car won't start, guilty for being late for work, anxious about the board meeting, and fearful about losing our jobs, all in less than one hour.

The ego doesn't know if we are sitting in our cars or running away from a group of coyotes. If we have a strong enough attachment to negative thoughts, the ego will create the same adverse feeling inside of us (like an animal instinct). For example, you give a dog a bone and instantly see a change in his or her demeanor. When you try to take the bone back from the dog, it will growl and show its teeth at you. It was a fun-loving doggy a second ago. The moment you give the dog the bone, the dog sees it as "my bone" and gets angry at anyone trying to take it from him or her. Just like if you were eating a piece of chocolate cake and someone came and tried to take it away from you, you would maybe get upset.

This is an innocent example showing the animal/survival mechanisms at work. Humans carry the same automatic reactions as the animal but with a more sophisticated and advanced brain. We have a major increased intelligence to go with the primitive ego, so we can advance above its limitations.

Today, the ego's natural and automatic reactions that occur in us are no longer necessary for survival. By continuing to hold onto these nonbeneficial qualities, we live through experiences of inner suffering in the form of shame, guilt, apathy, grief, fear, desire, and anger. Here is a general view of how animals needed the ego's reactions and natural instincts for survival: shame (to withdraw), guilt (to know an action was wrong through trial and error), apathy (to categorize enemies), grief (to learn how to not repeat dangerous situations), fear (to be aware of predators with a heightened sense of anxiety to initiate the fight-or-flight response), desire (to seek prey and food for survival and have the inner desire to find a mate), and anger (to protect themselves from enemies with adrenaline responses to get pumped up if needed to fight).

We can see how these responses were necessary to maintain survival in the animal kingdom. Without them, animals wouldn't be able to subsist. However, humans are not living in these primitive circumstances anymore, so we no longer need these engrained responses, which now only bring negativity, pain, and suffering into our lives.

These emotions are very common, and we experience them each day because the ego is built into our brains' mechanisms. The good news is that, once we understand more about the ego's automatic reactions, we can catch its primitive ways and begin to break down the source of our suffering. With the right knowledge, we can see why these responses are built into us and why it is clear we don't need them anymore.

Now let us explore common ways humans use the ego for nonsurvival purposes and introduce the ego's reactions into everyday life (which ultimately causes suffering):

- **Shame**. We feel embarrassed about something that happened, was said, or we feel is wrong about us. We feel humiliated when we attach to shame. It gives us low self-confidence and expectations. We feel like we are small while everything else is big and mighty.

- **Guilt**. We feel like we did something wrong, not acceptable by society. We blame ourselves for the reason something "bad" happened. We align with this ego-based characteristic to point fingers when we need to and to feel guilty when we get caught doing something wrong/bad.

- **Apathy**. Self-hatred and hatred for the world drowns apathy. People can get attracted to it when they feel like the ultimate victim. In this state, the feeling of despair overrides consciousness. We feel like nothing is going our way or something bad is always happening. **Grief**. Humans are overwelmed with this state when something happens and we regret not doing something we should have done before it happened. When someone passes away, we can feel grief. Some people are enslaved into this feeling when someone they really love passes away all of a sudden. This creates a missing piece in ourselves and causes severe inner suffering.

- **Fear**. Humans have taken the natural fear response that was created as a survival instinct to detect danger and elaborated it to the extreme in terms of the negativity and damage it has on our lives. We all have fears. We are afraid of dying and public speaking. We have materialistic fears like not having enough money, losing a job, getting sick, and so forth. The amount of energy that goes into fearful thinking strains our bodies and minds. Fear is definitely an aspect of survival. It was established to protect us. Now we fear something in anticipation that it will have a negative effect on our lives. Interestingly, most of our fears don't really put us in any real form of danger, but our elaborated perceptions of the fright cause us to feel the same negative emotion as if we were in actual serious danger. Fear sprouts when we have a strong opinion or position about something and the ego (false self) tells us it is worth panicking about because it seems like it will have a negative impact on our lives in the near or direct future. Although some fears are credible in the sense that they do provoke harm—like being afraid when a bear attacks you—being apprehensive when not in danger is obviously not necessary. It is more beneficial to be careful and aware of the potential danger without literally fearing it. The fact that a fear subsides when we don't focus on it proves that it itself is just a slanted way of thinking. A fear does not exist when we don't think and attach to it, yet it is one of the hardest things to surrender. When we find ourselves in the state of fear, it is hard to get out of it because we truly believe in what we dread. We become attached to the reasoning that tells us the fear is worth worrying about. It is a very debilitating and self-destructive way of experiencing the world because it overrides our consciousness and puts restrictions on our life potential. It is important to know that, other than real fear we experienced when something is trying to hurt us, all other fright just causes inner suffering and is unnecessary for our survival. We can be careful without being fearful.

- **Desire**. Most people have so many constant desires that we can't list them all. Desire in humans means to seek something from the external world that will provide a sense of happiness or fulfillment, for example, the desire for money, sex, a big house, a nice car, or a drug. A desire is anything we look upon externally to provide us with a feeling of betterment. Desires replace themselves with new ones, and no matter how much you give in to this emotion, it will never be satisfied. Some millionaires who have more money than an average person could spend in a lifetime still desire and crave more and more money. It doesn't matter how much they have. We can surrender desire when we realize sustained happiness and contentment will never come from an external source. All peace and happiness arise from within. Desire can be replaced with acceptance and joy for the moment instead of a longing for something in the future.

- **Anger**. Humans automatically get angry for one reason or another. We are the only species that literally gets pissed off if something does not go our way. Animals only get angry when their animal instincts tell them they have to protect something. Humans get angry for the sake of fuming. We get angry about work, coffee that isn't hot enough, or the TV remote not working. We can feel anger toward someone or something a person said. We can get angry about how something turned out or an object we can't control or get. Anger is a dangerous feeling because, when we are irate, we get an automatic adrenaline response that gets us pumped up and ends up making us do things we wouldn't normally do.

- **Pridefulness**. Unlike other force-based emotions, pride was not a basic animal instinct. It was established as the human species evolved. Pride is the emotion with which the majority of our societies choose to live in. Humans are proud all the time. It's not a bad emotion at all, and it feels good to be delighted with something. To be proud of something and to live in pridefulness are very different. When we are living in pride, we automatically form an opinion about everything, centralizing the world around ourselves and elaborating a sense of specialness in order to make us feel important. Pride scorns others and looks down at its surroundings when it feels the right to base on its pre-established opinions. Pride is envious, jealous, and competitive. It compares itself to everything else and feels the need to be better than everything else. When pride is put in the spotlight, stands naked, and finds itself humiliated or not projected in the way it wants others to see it, it can easily be forced into negative feelings such as anger and shame. This is why we must surrender pride in order to advance our inner growth and move toward a life of ongoing happiness that is not based on external events or the way the world views us. People feel that, if they surrender their pride, they will be less important and not as many people will care about them or see them in the way they want to be perceived. The exact opposite is true. Without pridefulness, we become more likeable, easygoing, sought after, and looked up to. For example, when we look at celebrities, we can see when pride overrides their consciousness simply by watching their actions and reactions to comments. When celebrities build themselves up to believe they are special, unique, and better than others, they come off as arrogant and less likeable nowadays. As a result, people pay less attention to prideful celebrities. On the other hand, celebrities who align with humility rather than pride become attractive, likeable, and looked up to as role models. Pride carries limitations and restrictions with it, and when surrendered, a new world of empowerment and opportunity to feel better arises. When we surrender pridefulness, we find courage. Instead of boasting ourselves up to being something we want others to see us as, we are thankful, grateful, and appreciative for our lives.

All of these emotions/feelings are completely natural, and it is normal to experience some on a daily basis. But the underlying fact is that each one of these emotions causes a certain degree of suffering due to the alignment with the false self (ego). The resulting inner distress restricts the experience of happiness in our lives. When our central focus is on any one of these negative feelings, they drain our positive energies and prevent us from the always present positive experience that is hidden behind the layers of negative emotions.

Surrendering the Ego

Life is like a garden; the beauty is limitless. The mind is sprouting weeds and flowers. When the mind stops sprouting and watering the weeds, the beauty of the garden is revealed, and the flowers are free to blossom.

All inner problems arise from the identification with the false self. We are free to the extent we are unrestricted from the ego. When the ego has no hold on our consciousness and is completely surrendered, the term "enlightenment" is used. Many mystics in history—such as Buddha, Gandhi, and Mother Teresa—became free from the ego's common reactions. The power of their energy is so radiant that almost everyone in the world still knows about them today.

Clearly, surrendering of the ego is the most important thing we can do in our lives for our own sake. Underneath the restraints of the ego lies great freedom. To unlock this independence, we realign with the spirit self instead of the false self.

To find freedom from inner suffering, we surrender the attachment we have to the thought processes and patterns that cause us negative emotions. By taking a step back and looking at our lives, we can notice different attachments between our thoughts and negative emotions. For example, we can feel anxious about one thing in our lives and guilty about another. A change in our thought patterns occurred. Our thoughts create the world we experience, and the ego holds our thought patterns in negativity. Surrendering the ego merely means yielding negative thought patterns.

It is hard to surrender the ego's hold without realizing, "I have the choice to change the pattern of my thoughts to create the resulting inner feelings I want to experience."

The ego hides behind the feeling that it is appropriate for us to feel a certain way now and a different condition later. Our favorite sports team won, so it is appropriate to feel happy. He yelled at me and called me a name, so it is fitting for me to feel anger. Usually when the ego tells us it is appropriate to feel a certain way, we listen to it. Why? When did it become appropriate for something to tell us whether it is appropriate to feel happy or not in the present moment? When did it become appropriate to hurt ourselves with negative thoughts and emotions? We deserve better. The ego's shadowing walls hide the beautiful reality of life. We see a life with restrictions. As we tear through the barriers, we will discover a life without limitations and full of peace and freedom.

People just want to feel inner contentment and peace. When you ask someone what he or she wants in this life, most people will say, "I just want to be happy and content and live a fulfilled life." In order to do so, we have to make the connection between "wanting to feel this" and "how to feel it." In order to feel good, we can't be constantly going over everything that our minds perceive as wrong.

When we alter what we focus on in our minds, our life experiences begin to mirror that change. Choose to focus on everything that is wonderful in your life. Replace fear with courage, anger with compassion, blame with forgiveness, shame with acceptance, grief with gratitude, and hate with love. Externals have no control over your inner feelings. All power lies with you.

Living in the Mind

It is easy to get caught up in thinking about something in the future, worrying about it, stressing about it, and thinking about how it will turn out, what will happen, and what it will be like. It is just as easy to find ourselves thinking about the past, regretting what happened, wishing it would have happened a different way, or believing we should have made a better decision.

When the mind is negatively focused on the worlds of past and future, it blocks our ability to experience the peace of living in the moment. The goal is to become free from worry of the past and anxiety of the future, to experience the freedom of living every moment to its fullest.

In our minds, we constantly project ourselves into the future in an effort to ensure our continued survival, and we seek some kind of betterment that will come later in life. When we do get a break from past or future thoughts, we turn on the live talk show in our minds and get distracted with the moment-to-moment talking mind commenting, rationalizing, judging, dictating, taking sides, and determining what is right and wrong according to us. This characteristic of our talking minds hide behind the perception of me. Because these are "my thoughts", they are worth listening to and making me feel the way they make me feel, even if they are negative and not making me feel good.

There are over seven billion people thinking right now in the world, blabbering away in their minds. Isn't this funny to think about? When we stop thinking about ourselves and focus on the bigger picture, life begins to become humorous. It's a good thing that thoughts are hidden, or it would be a very interesting world. People would have to be honest for once, or their true colors would show. If we could see what everyone was thinking about on a chart, their thoughts could be categorized into columns that illustrate the resulting emotions associated with all the different types of thoughts. People create their inner experience based on the thoughts they claim and defend as their own.

Many people zoom in on a specific negative point in their minds and then experience whatever they are thinking about. It is like the media. Every day, amazing things happen all around the world, but the media seems to ignore all of them and focus on a tiny fraction of chaos in the world, which ultimately instills fear. When was the last time we turned on the news and it said, "Today is a great day, the world is turning, the sun is shining, people are happy, and we have nothing to worry about"? If the media just did this, people would feel a little bit better and safe. It works the same in our minds. Once we zoom out from the negative focus point in our minds, we are free from that negativity. The more we do it, the easier it becomes.

People always think they have to do something in order to feel peace. The opposite is true. When we stop doing wrong, peace arises. Without the negative babbling going on in our minds, the inner experience is less stressful, and it becomes easier to simply enjoy the moment. We always have the choice to zoom out of negative thinking, become aware of being cognizant, and enjoy the feeling of being alive. When done, one is living in the moment instead of the mind.

The Ocean of Thoughts

Imagine a boat floating in water. The ocean surrounds the boat. The boat is you; the ocean is your thoughts. The thoughts you attach to it determine if the ocean is calm or if it has waves rocking your boat. Negative thinking toward others or ourselves bring on waves. The larger the attachment to the thought and feeling, the larger the wave one has to ride. You get to the point where you say, "That's enough. I am tired of these waves." So we look at what we can do to calm them.

At first, when we are trying to tame the waves (our thoughts), it may seem nearly impossible. Previous waves are still coming in from the past. If you don't want to have to experience these waves of emotion, ask yourself three questions: Am I creating a wave? Am I riding a wave? Am I calming the wave?

It is common to feel like we have to ride each thought or wave as it arises and experience the inner resulting experience. But we don't. We can calm the waves and create a new life for ourselves, one where our boats can effortlessly float through the water. When the boat stops rocking and we aren't bombarded with the turbulence, one is free to find contentment in the present experience. A realization arises. "Wow! This isn't that bad after all. I can't believe I could have been doing this all along!"

Once we find this contentment and we start to look around, we see all the other boats on the ocean that are riding waves of their own making as well. Some boats are overwhelmed with huge waves and are almost tipping over because the tide is so extreme. Others are relatively small, but still the boat is affected.

It becomes obvious that something needs to be done to help these boats. So a sail is raised high enough for all the boats who want to see it to read it. The sail's words simply read, "Stop creating waves if you don't want to have to ride them."

The Barking Dog

When a dog is moved to his new home, something startles him, and he starts barking. He continues to bark and bark until he gets to a point where he doesn't even know why he is barking anymore, but it has become so automatic and normal that he continues to bark, not even aware that the barking is why he is not relaxed and content.

The analogy with humans is that our spirits come to relax and find inner peace, but when we got here, something (our egos) startles us, and the negative thinking (barking) started. The negative thinking has continued for so long and become so automatic that we see it as normal.

When the dog realizes for just a moment that he doesn't have to keep barking anymore, the barking begins to fade. It will start and stop until the dog feels like it is more normal to just lie down and relax in silence instead of constantly barking. Likewise, when we realize we don't have to keep thinking all the time about every little thing that is happening or will occur in our lives, a peaceful silence begins to arise. When we stay aware what is going on in our minds and choose to detach with negative thought patterns, an inner content silence will eventually dominate. Now when we need the mind, we can activate it, and when we don't, we can let it be at peace.

Self-Awareness

What makes someone aware? Awareness is a quality of consciousness. People live their lives at different degrees of awareness. All human beings are cognizant in the sense that they stop when they come to a red light. And they go when the light turns green. This type of awareness is built into everyone. If it weren't, we wouldn't know we exist. But what does it mean to be self-aware? Are you?

Self-awareness means to be conscious of what is going on in your mind. It is the act of watching your thoughts. Without self-awareness, we are at the mercy of our minds because we are living the thoughts as they arise. With self-awareness, we have a choice about what we think about.

Thoughts are sneaky. They can take you to distant worlds in your mind. You can be having a fight in your head about something that happened at work while eating supper. This is called "sleeping." You probably have experienced this sometime in your life, both firsthand and in some of the people around you. It is like being lost in your imagination. People are so caught up in a distant thought that they are unable to enjoy the present moment or even be aware of it. This is apparent when you are driving home from work and you look over to someone driving his or her car. Some people almost look in a zombie state because they are so consumed by their thoughts racing through their heads from the day's experiences.

Self-awareness is so important in the process of finding inner freedom. Only when self-awareness is achieved can we start making a change in our inner lives. When we are aware of arising thoughts, we have the choice how or if we want to react to those contemplations. The more self-aware one becomes, the greater capacity to grow the inner being and expand one's consciousness.

As self-awareness progresses, it becomes a burden to react to every little thought. Instead, thoughts pass uninterrupted by the individual. Eventually, the needless perceptions fade away. A thought's only power is the one you give it. If you entertain the thought, it will entertain you. We are not our thoughts. They are only a part of us. Through practice and introspection, one can become the master of the mind instead of a slave to it.

Wherever you are, be present there, and give it your full, undivided attention. Live in the state of being aware that you are. When a thought comes up to try to lead you astray, surrender it just as fast as it arises. The goal is to live in the present moment and be aware of all arising thoughts. When an unnecessary perception arises and says, "Here I am! Listen to me," you can say back to it, "No thanks! I'd rather not go there." If you catch yourself doing this, you are well on your way. This is what is called "being mind awake."

In each moment, you are aware of not only your thoughts but also yourself witnessing them. When you reach this point of watching yourself witness the thoughts, you can choose what you think about to determine your inner experience. To be awakened is to be free. The great enlightened Buddha taught, "What we think, we become." (Founder of Buddhism, 563-483 B.C). Gandhi said, "A man is but the product of his thoughts. What he thinks, he becomes." (Mahatma Gandhi, 1869-1948).

Creating Your Inner Reality

Life is experienced inside of us. Nothing in our lives has been experienced outside of ourselves. Have you ever undergone something outside of your inner experience? No. You see things outside of yourself, but the experience you have is still within. Think about it very closely until you get that "aha" moment.

Nothing is experienced out there, and it never has. All that has happened from the moment you were born up until this very moment was a variety of changing inner experiences that range from being exciting, satisfying, joyful, pleasant, and content to being frustrated, sad, maddening, and other different forms of unpleasantness. So the real question is, "What is constantly changing inside of us that is altering the way we feel?"

The answer is our perceptions, the way we see what is happening around us. The change in feeling is a direct result in how we perceive something to be occurring, for example:

- We feel pleasant to different degrees when we slant our perceptions to believe that what is going on is good.
- We feel unpleasant when we slant our perceptions to believe what is going on is bad or no good.

Depending on how much we choose to slant our perceptions in either direction determines if we have a really good or bad inner feeling or something in between.

This is why the awareness to thoughts and their patterns that are taking place inside of our minds is the most important step in the process of making yourself feel better. One must stay consciously aware, but it's not just for a moment. We are to forever stay aware of the contents of the mind and the way it is making you feel in every instant. If you are not aware of your thoughts, they can run all over you. You become a slave to your own mind. No one wants to be a slave to anything, right? So what do you say we stop letting the mind control our feelings!

If you are serious about feeling better and changing your inner experience to a positive, everlasting experience, then you become willing to look what is happening inside your own mind. You adjust your thought patterns and outward intentions so they benefit your well-being.

Thoughts can be your best friend or enemy. When perceptions have a negative slant to them, they are hurtful to you and restrict you from inner well-being. It is like you become the punching bag and the thoughts are the fists doing the punching. On the other hand, when they have a positive slant to them, they are beneficial to your well-being.

How willing are you to change all your thoughts to positive? Is it worth your happiness? If you are unwilling to change your thoughts for the better, then you are saying to yourself, "I am unwilling to let myself be happy." It is just like saying, "My thoughts are more important than my happiness." Is a thought more important than letting yourself feel good? Is anything more key than your happiness? Nope.

Focus on your inner happiness. All else distracts you. If happiness is the most important thing in your life, what are you willing to do to achieve inner happiness? Are you willing to

- release thoughts that deny you from being happy;
- be conscious of yourself and what is going on at each moment in your mind;
- change negative slants to positive; or
- release the knee-jerk reaction that tells you it is okay to respond in a negative manner in certain circumstances?

If we are willing to hold ourselves to these, we will have no problem finding happiness and peace of mind.

If a negative thought pattern is consistent and you are finding it hard to let go, ask yourself, "Why am I giving my attention to this thought? Why do I think this thought is important?" When you shine a light on negative thoughts, they scurry away like rats. When you resist anything, you experience it.

Take a third-person view and relate with your thoughts in that manner. This greatly helps because, the moment the thought goes from "my thought" to "just a thought," it turns from being seen as important because it is mine to not important and not worth holding onto because it is just a thought that is causing me to feel worse when I think about it.

Anytime thoughts are giving you a hard time, realize it is not worth holding onto because it is just a thought and you didn't create it. You know it is actually your thought when it is aligned with making you feel good. At the same time you are thinking about anything, probably thousands or millions of other people in the world are thinking similar thought patterns and feeling the same because of it. Therefore, thoughts that cause stress do not deserve your attention. Focus your attention on your happiness, not passing thoughts that distract you from your happiness.

Maintain your inner attention to every thought that goes through your mind and the way it is making you feel in that moment. Anything that doesn't feel quite right or good, surrender it instantly. It doesn't feel good for a reason. It is an indicator built into us to warn us that the way we are relating to something is not correct and the thought doesn't belong in our consciousness. Your feelings are your own inner teacher. Listen to your feelings and what they are telling you.

If you want to be happy and content, don't let anything that is nonbeneficial to your experience into your mind. Only allow that which will set you free from negativity and uplift your experience of life. It just makes sense. Not many people realize we can think about anything we want to at any moment. If we did, why would we think about anything that is negative and causes suffering? The spectrum of the mind is open to all possible mentalizations. We can think about anything. So why does the mind zero in on the very few negative aspects of our lives?

The simple truth is that the ego is actually addicted to focusing on the negative. If it wasn't, it wouldn't do it. So one easy way to figure out if you are identifying with the ego or spirit is to simply examine in that moment what type of thought you are holding onto and what you are feeling inside. If it contains any sort of negativity, the ego brought you to that thought. If it is positive and uplifting, the spirit brought you to it. Let your spirit live through your mind. Let your heart decide what you think about. That's all that needs to be done. Your spirit knows what is best for you. Let it guide you into the direction of your well-being. The ego can go jump on a trampoline or something and amuse itself somewhere else. It is time for the spirit to awaken and take you for a ride of inner pleasure. But before it can do that, you must make an inner decision to let go of holding onto any form of negativity.

Embrace the transformation from ego mind to spirit mind. Be excited about the opportunity and the positive change that can be experienced with just a simple change in perception.

Backpack of Thoughts

See thoughts a different way for a moment. Imagine you are wearing a backpack. Every negative thought you attach to in your mind, a heavy block is added to your backpack and weighs you down. Too many negative thoughts (blocks) make your feel burdened, weigh you down, restrict your movement, cause suffering, and create illness. Even though thoughts are not visible, they are very real in the power they carry and the way they affect the physical body and inner life experience.

There is a way to remove negative blocks holding you back. Every positive thought and affirmation that is held in the mind, lets say ten blocks are removed from your backpack. Positive is tenfold more powerful than negative. With continuous, sincere positive thinking backed by positive intention, all the negative weights can be removed from your backpack. Once all are released from the backpack via not letting negative thoughts be a part of your inner experience and replacing the mind activity with positive intentions, you will be free to drop the backpack and leave it behind. You will realize, why was I holding onto the backpack of negativity in the first place.

Now that the backpack that holds negativity is no longer carried with us because we have realized negative thinking is not necessary for our survival, positive thoughts can start having a full effect on our consciousness. With each new positive and uplifting thought and affirmation, peace flows directly into the human being. If one is devoted to this, more and more liberating and uplifting peace can be added to the human being's experience. This is only possible when mind negativity is surrendered and the backpack of suffering is let go. We are the sole controller of what goes into our backpacks or if we are carrying one at all.

Negative thinking is also like putting heavy homework books into our backpacks that we have to attend to later. You lug them around everywhere you go and wonder why life is not full of joy. A massive weight is on your shoulders, and it is not letting you express yourself to your full potential. People even treat thought-based negativity like homework in the sense it is not just a passing thought. They go back to it, open the book later, and focus their inner attention onto it. If you focus on any sort of negativity, you are forced to feel it. Nobody likes homework anyway (negative thinking). We should get to the point that we are so fed up with the never ending cycle, that we are willing to drop it for good.

One by one, remove the heavy homework from your backpack with a positive mind, thoughts, and affirmations. The power of positive thinking is so much more powerful than negative thoughts. Thank God. So it is actually very easy to remove the weights, but only when the individual has made the inner choice that he or she wants to do so and has the willpower and dedication to follow through. Once you have made the choice, maintain this new way of living in the mind for more than just ten minutes or an hour. Doing it for such a short time will only cause frustration and disappointment. Do this inner practice for five days, and watch the miracle that takes place. It doesn't even take that long.

How many days have you lived so far? If you figure out this amount, five days or less of trying something new to see if it can help you for the rest of your life seems worth it. Call it the five days to inner well-being. Through the process, you will see a positive change take place, a weight will be lifted off your shoulders, inner contentment will become more consistently present in your life, and you will feel free to express yourself to your full potential without some unknown force clouding the way. After doing it this practice of surrending negatively as it arises consistently, it becomes an automatic way of being and requires no effort at all.

CHAPTER 3

UNIVERSAL ENERGY

This chapter focuses on the universal energy that governs our internal experiences. It elaborates on the power of thoughts and the field of consciousness that connects all of life.

Thought Energy

If thoughts have power, how would you use it? Would you be throwing away your power, or would you choose carefully how you used it? What if the very thoughts that go on in our minds can either strengthen or weaken people as well as ourselves? Would you then think differently about what is going on in your own mind?

Think about how powerful thoughts can be just from experience. When you think about something you hate or dislike, it has the power to make you feel upset and angry. When you think about something you love, you feel content and happy. Thoughts are a form of power. This is verifiably proved with applied muscle testing kinesiology where it shows the effect thoughts have on the human system.[1] The short version of applied muscle testing

---

[1]   You can find more information and experiments to show this in detail on the Internet or books related to the subject, such as *Power vs. Force* (1995).

kinesiology is when someone holds out his or her arm to the side. Someone else thinks of a positive thought, says "resist," and tries to push down on the arm. The subject goes strong. When someone thinks of a negative thought, says "resist," and pushes down on the arm, the subject's arm goes weak and is unable to stay strong.

This tells us two very important facts:

- Thoughts have energy.
- They affect everything around them.

So when you are living your life and thinking with positive intentions (for the better), you make the people's energy field around you go strong. Just as well when a thought has a negative intention (for the worse), people's energy field around you weaken. It is also a fact. Everyone is connected. If we weren't, such applied muscle testing kinesiology would not be possible. All is connected in the universe by the field of consciousness and shares the same underlying awareness.

You can see a thought as a unit of energy that carries with it the capacity to make us experience the energy it holds. This energy arises out of nothingness (the ocean of thoughts) and forms a pattern and intention that determines the feeling that comes with it. Negative thoughts carry adverse energy that spreads throughout our bodies and minds and causes suffering and illness. Positive thoughts carry affirmative energy, which works to heal and benefit our bodies and minds. The human brain releases endorphins and feel-good hormones when we think kind, compassionate, and loving thoughts. So this is not just talk. It actually feels good to think positive.

Each intention, thought, action, and word carries a physical energy with it that is either positive or negative and can be clearly witnessed in everyday life. For example, when someone says something nice to you with words of positive intention, that affirmative energy is transferred to you and makes you feel uplifted. On the contrary, when someone says something negative toward you, you internalize that adverse energy and have an immediate response to react to it with an equally damaging force. This is the law of force equals force.

To stop pain and suffering for others and ourselves, we must first change what is going on inside of us. We choose to attach to the positive energies that can be easily found through willingness, acceptance, forgiveness, kindness, thankfulness, and love. In every situation, we are given the decision to choose kindness over anger, thankfulness over frustration, happiness over disappointment, and love over hate. We dedicate ourselves to choosing the positive over the negative in every situation. When we do, inner suffering subsides. Things that bothered you before will have absolutely no effect on you. The real proof will come by witnessing the change. With every positive action, thought and intention, you change your life for the better and change the world more than could ever be imagined or seen.

The Field of Consciousness

At the beginning of the book, we discussed consciousness and how everything that exists has it. To further elaborate on the subject, we will look into the field in which all consciousness is connected. The common belief is as an individual we are separate from everything else when, in reality, we are all connected in the universe.

Thinking we are disconnected from everything has limited our perceptions of reality. We automatically believe the thoughts that go on in our minds are only ours, and they have no reality outside of ourselves. It is a scientific fact that this is not true.

The most advanced quantum physics sciences tell us that a field of consciousness or a divine matrix connects all living things. The field of consciousness is the container for the entire universe. It is a bridge between our inner worlds and all of life. It is the conduit that connects what is going on inside us to the effects it has on everything in the universe.

The field of consciousness records all thoughts, actions, and intentions and reflects them back to us. It is like a mirror that shines back to us what we feel in our hearts. To get a better explanation, I highly recommend looking into Gregg Braden's book, *The Divine Matrix*.

We assumed the intentions of our thoughts were hidden from the world, but they are actually picked up into the field of consciousness and reflected back at us without exception.

What does this mean? People are the power. Human emotions and inner feelings literally have an effect on the world. People have the power to change the world and uplift mankind. When we have negative intentions, we adversely affect the overall field of consciousness. When we have positive intentions, we lift the field of consciousness and make the world a better place for everyone. This is why you literally change the world by what you have become.

Understanding this one key point gives us a greatly enhanced understanding about life. The field of consciousness is the ever-present mirror in our lives. It reflects back what we send out. So in order to experience an internal change of well-being, we first must change our inner intentions and thoughts to that of compassion, forgiveness, and love. Once we live in these feelings, the mirror of life will shine back the same positive energy that we sent up into the field. This is where sayings like "You get what you put out" and "When you smile, the world smiles back" come into play. It is how the mirror of life was designed. The field of consciousness will let you see the world you choose to perceive and experience the world you choose to face by reflecting back what you send out into the world.

Effect of Energy

Energy has a domino effect that spreads to others. For example, Bob wakes up in the morning, and he is in a bad mood for one reason or another. He gets up and, right away, has nothing nice to say. He gets angry at his children and his wife, yells at other drivers who cut him off, and disrespects his secretary and employees. The effects of this negative energy do not stop with Bob. His children go to school feeling disappointed and angry, and in turn, they act out negatively toward teachers and students. Bob's wife stays home alone and bathes in feelings of sadness and self-judgment. The kids come home from school, and Mom doesn't feel very good, so she is unable to give the kids the positive environment they seek.

The negative domino effect continues. Bob's secretary and employees feel angry, unnoticed, and unappreciated for the hard work they do each day. They get home, and the negative aspects of work life do not let them feel happy or content about their lives because they have to go to work the next day, which causes them to not treat their families with the right appreciation and so on.

The negative domino effect continues as each person is exposed to the negative energy and spreads it to others, whether he or she knows it or not. This is because, due to the law of force, when a negative force is applied, an equally adverse reaction occurs unless a higher power intervenes. When Bob gets home to his wife and kids, no one is happy to see him, and the negative energy has found its way back to Bob. He doesn't feel like his family appreciates the hard work he does for them, and he ends up feeling like the victim. No matter what energy (good or bad) you send out to the world, it always finds its way back to you. People can term this any way they like. Some commonly refer to it as karma.

Let's review the example again, this time in a positive light. Let's say Bob wakes up happy and filled with joy and love. He gives his wife and kids a big smile and tells his family how proud he is of them and how much he loves them. He leaves for work, leaving his wife and children in an uplifted mood, ready to take on the day ahead. The children are filled with joy and excitement as they learn new things at school because they know they will be safe and loved when they return home. Bob's wife feels respected and thankful for her loving husband and children. Bob gets to work and feels great. He gives all of his employees a big smile, respects them, and conveys how much he appreciates them for the hard work they put in each day. As a result, his employees work harder for the company because they know their efforts are appreciated. Bob's secretary and employees are happy and bring this happiness home with them to spread to their families and friends.

The positive domino effect of one person has a profound effect on the world, and it continues to spread each day. As we become more self-aware, it is hard—if not impossible—to not be kind in every situation because we can literally see the positive effects unfolding before our eyes.

In the positive example, Bob gets home, and a loving, happy, healthy, and excited family welcomes him home. His wife prepares a nice dinner for him, and she is happy to do so. In return for his kindness and lovingness, he now receives all of their love. He goes to bed with inner contentment and a feeling of a fulfilled life. If Bob remains living in this positive energy, all aspects of his life will change for the better. No matter where he goes, his family, friends, and former enemies will always be excited to see him, and he will feel the respect and love of others in his heart.

For every positive action, you will experience an equally affirmative response. For every negative action, you will experience an equally adverse response. You get exactly what you put out into the world. No one is exempt from this universal law, no matter what he or she believes. Dedicating one's life to serving others by spreading the positive energy will have an immediate affirmative and life-changing effect. A good rule to follow is to never say, do, or think anything that you wouldn't want sent to you. Give to the world what you want to experience. Seems fair enough.

Energy Fields

There are two worlds: the one we see and the invisible world of energy fields. The domain we see and the individuals involved are operating under the influence of the world of energy fields.

So far in the book, we have discussed many factors that determine the inner experience, including one's alignment with spirit, degrees of awareness, and feelings brought on by outgoing reactions. Now let's move onto what determines how each person overall relates with the world.

Energy fields, fields of energy that consciousness is attracted to that determine the overall experience of life, determine the experience of individual consciousness. We choose to relate to the world in a certain way. An overall feeling prevails as the primary experience of one's consciousness based upon this choice. The overall energy field of its consciousness directly influences the inner thoughts of the individual. This is why some people are living in anger and have many irate thoughts. Others are living in desire and have several thoughts of craving. The field of energy that consciousness chooses to reside in accounts for the general expression of arising thoughts and the way they will react to situations.

The energy field experienced associates itself with specific thought patterns and ways of seeing the world. Along with every thought, intention, word, and action, it also carries with it energy, and the power it holds also attracts the energy fields that surround our individual consciousness. This makes us experience the inner world the way it is. It becomes a cycle. The energy fields attract specific thoughts, and the thoughts attract the energy field. It is hard to leave the energy field we are living in because it requires intervention from a higher energy field or thought patterns and intentions in order to expand one's conscious experience.

The overall energy field that surrounds us determines our behaviors, the way we react to situations, and the reason why we feel the way we do. We change the energy field that surrounds our consciousness by the way we choose to overall relate with the world. Basically, the relationship we have between our selves and the world attracts the energy field into our lives.

What are the energy fields? Falsehood energy fields include shame, guilt, apathy, grief, fear, desire, anger, and pridefulness. Truth energy fields include courage, neutrality, willingness, acceptance, reason, love, joy, and peace.

All thoughts based on falsehood surround us with a negative energy field. Living in falsehood energy fields cause inner suffering to different degrees. Its energy is demanding on us, and when held onto for too long, we can feel like walking time bombs with nowhere to release it. The lower the energy field we live in, the more pressure we put on our selves. Consciousness becomes a filter of that energy field, and it becomes the dominating experience of its life.

All thoughts and intentions based on truth align consciousness with a positive energy field. Truth energy fields are powerful and create neutral, content, and enjoyable inner experiences. One becomes a positive filter and generally reacts to situations based on the dominating energy field. So a person who is at the level of acceptance finds it easier to accept the happenings around him or her, and he or she doesn't let it disturb his or her inner world.

People act the way they do because they are living in specific energy fields that directly influence the overall inner experience, actions, and the way they relate with the world. Although people's actions can seem very random and chaotic at times, when we perceive it in terms of energy fields, it becomes quite clear why people are the way they are. It becomes easier to accept people for their way of being because we can now see them as a consciousness residing itself in a certain energy field and don't know how to get out of it.

If you find yourself stuck in any of the falsehood energy fields above, replace it with a more suitable field that is aligned with truth. With this knowledge, we can move up the scale of consciousness faster than ever and greatly improve our potentials for inner growth.

Changing Energy Fields

For anyone who wants to change the dominating energy field he or she is experiencing, you can do an exercise that will be effective in rebalancing your energy field. First, look at the list in the previous section, and pick out the energy field that you believe you are currently residing in. Various aspects of your life can be aligned with different energy fields, but choose the one you relate to most. Be honest with yourself for the best results. No energy field is better than another is. They are just different areas that consciousness can experience. Whichever energy field you believe to be the dominating one in your life, ask yourself,

"Am I happy living in this energy for the rest of my life?" If the answer is no, let's see what we can do to change the dominating energy field to one that is more enjoyable because you deserve a positive inner experience.

It starts with your inner world and the way you choose to be a filter to everything. Life gives us the chance to react to life, and by this very response, we are determining the energy field that surrounds us. So if you want to change the energy field, alter how you filter life through you. The easiest way to do this is to start by doing it for one hour, like an exercise.

Become willing to accept everything for the way it is for just an hour. Every time you are presented an opportunity to react to something, react with acceptance. Remove the old filter system—whether it was fear, desire, anger, and so forth—and put it to the side. We don't need that right now.

This is an exercise, and it requires it to be done consistently to get results. Just like if you were exercising to get into physical shape, consistency is key, and it's the exact same to get into inner shape. Just as you would only see results if you stay on the treadmill, this will only work if you remain in the new energy field. It doesn't work if you jump on and off the treadmill. Can you imagine seeing someone working out in the gym, seeing him or her running around from one machine to another, and only staying on each machine for a few moments? No progress would be getting done. He or she would just be wasting his or her time, and would be tired and frustrated in the process. It works the same here.

We can see an energy field like a workout machine. It doesn't work if you jump from fear to acceptance to shame to acceptance to anger to acceptance and so forth. If you remain in the field of acceptance, you will see quite fast progress. This means accepting of yourself, others, and all else.

If you stay aware of yourself and filter your reactions with acceptance without fail for an hour, you will start to change the energy field that surrounds your being. If you find it hard to be accepting of everything for the duration of the hour, you can replace it with neutral. So instead of automatically filtering life through you as you normally do, stay consciously aware and become neutral, meaning no good or bad reaction takes place toward yourself, people, or anything. Practice until it becomes automatic. Some find this easier, and it works great as well. In actuality, any truth-based energy field will work if you remain in it. For people who want to speed up the process, react to everything with love. It is not impossible and definitely the most rewarding. The energy field of love is a feeling of safeness, comfort, and completeness, and when the energy field is present, it is quite apparent.

After you have done the hour exercise, it is up to you how you wish to remain experiencing life. It is a fact that you will find more peace with the higher energy fields. It only requires effort to change the dominating energy field. Once the new energy field is dominant, that new experience becomes automatic without doing anything.

It really comes down to the individual, what feels natural to him or her and how willing he or she is to make or experience a change. If it helps, think of yourself as just one in seven billion. You don't need to be the one determining if everything is right or wrong and reacting based on that choice with a seemingly appropriate response. Enough people are doing that already. Instead, just focus on perfecting your inner experience and not letting anything take away your energy field of well-being from you.

CHAPTER 4

PERSPECTIVES OF LIFE

Relating with life from different perspectives opens our minds to new ways of seeing the world and ourselves.

External World vs. Internal World

There are two worlds: the external and internal. Western civilization is mainly focused on the external world of acquiring material things, living in a big house, having a nice car, and so forth. Abundance is great, and there is nothing wrong with it, but it becomes a problem when we are so focused on the acquisition of success in the external world that we fail to recognize what is going on inside of us. In Western society, being successful is primary over anything else because the belief is that happiness will follow once we have everything. Inner feelings are placed secondary. Does that make sense? Shouldn't it be the other way around? Should we not be focused on perfecting our inner experiences first so that, no matter what happens in our lives, we will be prepared and able to maintain a sense of inner contentment and peace? The external world will always be unpredictable and out of our control. The only area of our lives that we have complete control is what is going on inside of us. We control this, and when we take full responsibility and start living like we do, betterment will come into our lives.

Our ways of living have been constantly progressing for thousands of years. Today, we live in a world that looks quite civilized from the outside. Technology that once never could have been imagined to be possible is here in today's world, such as electricity and the recent introduction of the World Wide Web. When we look back at history and see how others used to make a living, our modern ways look extremely sophisticated. Technology and discoveries continue to rise to new heights, and the world we see will rapidly advance into a more futuristic way of living. This is exciting, but it can become a distraction to our inner growth. We become so absorbed into the world around us that we don't look within. What are the consequences of solely focusing on external happiness?

Children are born into a superficial world where external success is considered more important than how you feel. The illusion is that you will feel good once you have succeeded. And so the parade of life begins. Kids are taught everything they need to know to succeed in the world. When the time comes and they have to work, they can handle their responsibilities and sustain an income to raise a family. The desire for success keeps them going. They have an image of a day in their mind where everything will be perfect and innocently work toward that day. They justify their inner experience not being perfect in the present moment. Years go by, and life takes on its daily routine until one either gets fed up or finds himself or herself at that day he or she has been waiting for his or her entire life with everything he or she has ever been desiring when the questions arises. "Is this it? I still don't feel complete. What is wrong?" Depression sinks in. People turn to drugs or other external desires and start going to great lengths to find some sort of happiness out there in the world. This is because the illusion success is out there in the world when it is actually right here in our hearts.

Remember when there were no cars, airplanes, cell phones, big-screen TVs, GPS systems, electronic game systems, music players, DVD players, or Internet? When we look at it now, we ask, "How did they survive? What did they do to be happy?"

For some people, it would seem impossible to live without cell phones in their hands. The fact is that, even without all these toys, the mind would still be caught up in the same problems, and life wouldn't seem very different at all. Only we wouldn't be so distracted to realize something isn't quite right in our inner worlds. Even with all this cool technology, most people still feel an inner sense of not being complete and fully satisfied.

Advertisements for this new toy and gadget surround us, and through them, we can be tempted to seek a temporary sense of happiness from external sources. Without knowing it, the media and advertisements are brainwashing the mind, feeding into the illusion that the source of happiness is based on externals. We are led to believe our internal worlds depend on the external world, when in reality, our internal world actually determines the experience of the external world.

Our lives are set up around an external business marketplace, which allows our economies to sustain growth and lets us maintain our ways of living. This economic-based marketplace system seems to have distracted the majority of society from the ultimate goal, the reason we were born in the first place, to better our experiences and become something greater than we were previously with knowledge and life experiences to help us evolve.

Our lives can be so focused on materials and content, looking for something in the external world to satisfy our needs and constantly distracting ourselves that we are unable to ever find any real sense of peace. We end up feeling like a victim for one reason or another. In truth, we are. However, we are victims of the illusion that happiness is outside of ourselves.

In order to create a better experience, we realign our lives' compasses and start focusing on obtaining happiness from within. It is time to realize the potential of our inner technologies as human beings. The moment we become honest with ourselves and stop looking at external things to juice our joys and start focusing on perfecting our internal worlds, we will have taken the necessary step to discover the true powers of the internal world. From there, we can begin to change the way we react to everything else and stop waiting for everything else to bend its ways and align just perfect for us. This is one of the most important steps to finding true inner happiness because it all starts with us and the way we see and react to everything else.

Underlying Perspectives

The perspective we take in life can either restrict our growth or help us through the journey. It is beneficial to take responsibility for our own lives and the way we live them and realize we are the sole determining factor, which determines if we are using this life for the growth of our consciousness or delaying the process.

Life can be a miracle or a struggle. It is all about the perspective we choose to take. Having the right viewpoints on life is crucial in the process of inner growth. To find those that are beneficial to us, we seek knowledge to better understand life. When we find it hard to get over something, we look at it from a different point of view so we can see it a different way that allows us to move on and maintain our well-being.

Many views can blind us from reality and cause unnecessary worrying and suffering. These common perspectives limit our views on life, along with their truth counterparts in parenthesis:

1. I am separate from God. (God is within me; I am connected with the universe.)
2. I am the victim. (I am the miracle of life.)
3. No one loves me. (Creation unconditionally loves me.)
4. What is the point if we just die? (I live forever in eternity as spirit.)
5. I can't accept that happening to me. (You agreed to the test for inner growth.)
6. The world isn't fair. (Divine law governs all.)
7. Some people are bad, so I can judge them. (Consciousness is at different levels of awareness. To judge someone is to judge the evolution of life.)
8. I can't forgive myself; therefore, I hold onto my guilt. (Replace guilt with regret, ask life for forgiveness, and remove all inner guilt toward oneself for it is attracting an energy field of suffering. To know something is wrong and know you won't do it again is the life lesson. You already passed.)
9. I am small and unworthy. (You are consciousness, the most powerful thing in the universe.)
10. That person got away with wrongdoing. (People are accountable for their own karma.)

What Is Karma?

When people use the quote "Everything happens for a reason," it is a hard concept to grasp. Some situations and events seem too tragic to happen for any justifiable reason. The problem lies in a lack of understanding about how life works. People loosely refer to the term "karma" when they see something happen to someone after that person did something to deserve it. People say, "Well, that's karma!" and kind of laugh at it when it is not happening to them.

Truthfully, karma works like that but on a far greater scale. As spirit beings, we carry the karma we have collected through various lifetimes. It is like a backpack filled with all of our baggage that we carry. As spirits, we don't want to transport this on our backs so we reincarnate to free ourselves. This is just an analogy. So sometimes, what happens in this life is a result of something we did previously, and we want to release it from our soul and move on so we can grow.

Karma is divine law. Everything is recorded in the field of consciousness, so nothing is missed or not seen. People are responsible for their intentions and actions. This knowledge is necessary to know for many reasons. For one, it helps us relinquish judgment. We don't have to be the ones determining what is right and wrong and judge based on that. Life already knows what is taking place. We don't need to interfere.

This information is not to create fear about something bad we think we did and fear we are going to be punished from it. It doesn't work like that. Life is all forgiving, and there is no one to judge you or your actions other than yourself. The world can be a tough place to live as we all know, and everyone is just doing the best he or she can with the knowledge he or she has available. Be easy on yourself. We all make mistakes, and that is the process of life. Not one human being since the beginning of humanity has been absolutely perfect in his or her actions from the beginning of his or her life to the end, and that is a fact.

We can see earth as like the karma depot. Human life is an expression of divine grace and infinite mercy. It is an absolute gift to be born a human because it gives us the opportunity to balance our karma. Earth is where bad karma is dropped and good karma is collected. So it is like the backpack being replaced with wings so we can fly free. This is actually the sole purpose of life. We go through traumatic life experiences to release our bad karma or learn a life lesson that will be beneficial for our soul. We agreed to partake in the process because we know it is for our own benefits in the greater picture. Earthly life is just a fraction of our eternal existence.

There is no use going through life always judging what is good and bad and what is wrong and right because everything is happening for far greater reasons than our understanding. We are here to simply witness life with no judgment, undo bad karma, learn about who or what we are, and grow our consciousness to the extent we feel safe to love.

Life Tests

We can see everything and every situation in life as a test for our inner growth. We face the greatest problems in our lives because they are our greatest lessons to be learned in order to advance our inner growth. The harder the test seems, the greater the lesson to be learned.

When someone is having a hard time with something in his or her life and directs that negative energy toward you, it is a test. How will you react? It is a test when someone cuts you off in traffic or steals or damages something of yours. And so on and so on from the most extreme to the simplest of tests. We can pass each test with flying colors with the right awareness, attitude and perspective, no matter how many fails we got in the past. Actually, life gradually becomes increasingly humorous, and you look forward to your tests so you can show them who is boss.

We pass the tests by choosing to have positive intentions over the negative in each situation, accept someone instead of hating him or her, and react responsibly from within, no matter how much the mind says it is worth getting worked up about.

The world had to be this way for the evolution of life to progress as it should. The only way we can grow is if life has been set up exactly the way it is in the form of these life tests that present us with choices. They are not so much tests as they are opportunities.

Often we wish we could change many aspects of our lives or go back in time and erase. Or we wish they had never happened at all or weren't going to happen in the future. This constant thought process of trying to edit and change what is happening in the world causes us inner suffering and pain. Acceptance is freeing.

Instead of trying to edit life, we witness the miracle of life and gift of experiencing it in the first place. The following statement is a good perspective we can adopt to help us maintain a positive outlook on life. "My life is a miracle. The moment of being alive in each instance and the ability for me to be aware is complete in itself. Everything else is a bonus."

The Miracle of Life

You are experiencing the miracle of life. We live in a perfect world where the miraculous is the commonplace. If we imagine everything that has to take place at each instance in order for us to experience this moment of awareness, it is quite remarkable. Where do we begin? First, we need an Earth with the essential properties to maintain living conditions such as water. We need a universe to sustain the Earth. We need the laws of the universe to maintain synchronicity and balance so the Earth can move through space at a consistent rate of speed while maintaining gravity and stillness within its atmosphere. Then we need the physical laws of the Earth.

And the miracle continues. The sun shines down on Earth at a perfect distance to provide light, nurturing, and warmth for our survival. Clouds form so the rain can fall. Fruits, vegetables, flowers, trees, and grass grow from the combination of nutrients from the earth. The sun's rays and the rain fall from the sky. Animals of all types of different species establish in various habitats and become units of the cycle of life as well as sacrifice their life as a food source for humans. If any piece of the cycle of life were missing, including you, the entire puzzle would fall apart.

Not only is there an established and functional earth that flies through space at high speeds of rotation, we also get to experience living inside the swirling earth. To be alive in this perfect world is an absolute miracle, and to be living as a human in this moment is a gift beyond all words. We are exactly where we wanted to be in this moment. When we break down what it means to be alive, we can see how blessed we really are. We get to make friends, laugh, create memories, feel love, establish families, experience awareness, and grow our inner spirits.

Everything plays its part in the miracle of life—the Earth, the universe, the sun, the moon, the clouds, the animals, the humans, and all else—to make this experience possible. Humans are aware of the experience of life. Not only are we cognizant of it, we get to undertake living on this earth with inner feelings and emotions. As the massive Earth rotates through space, each human being's life is maintained in the middle of it all, and he or she is experiencing an inner world of his or her own making. The experience can either be positive or negative depending on how we are relating with life.

The miracle continues. Have you ever noticed that everything is also intrinsically beautiful in its design? Beauty is all around us. Humans, animals, rivers, forests, sunsets, and flowers are attractive. Everything is stunning because it was purposely designed that way.

The miracle doesn't end there. We have eyes to see the beauty in 3-D color. We have ears to hear the sounds. We have lungs so we can breathe. We have a mind so we can think. We have legs so we can walk. We have arms and hands so we can pick up things. We have a tongue so we can taste food. We have vocal chords so we can communicate. We can procreate. We have emotions so we can feel love. What else do we want?

Noticing the perfection of the miracle and what it takes in order for us to experience each and every moment can put us into a new paradigm. It broadens our minds and opens the path to an expansion of greater perception. Once we become aware of the miracle, we can be thankful. We can change our worries and disappointments and replace them with an appreciation and respect for life and creation.

If you look at everything as if you were seeing it for the first or last time, you will see the miracle. As you blink and take each new breath, relax and know you are being taken care of and the energy of life will take care of you. Creation unconditionally loves everything in the miracle of life, or it wouldn't exist in the first place.

God View

Depending on where we choose to position ourselves in life, the view of God changes. To the ego, the views of God are based on falsehood because the ego itself is based on this concept. The ego stands for "Edge God Out" (Dr. Wayne Dyer). Why? So it can be its own version of God for the limited time it has here on earth. The perspective of God from the lower viewpoints of the ego includes a despising, vindictive, condemning, uncaring, punitive God. These are all false depictions of God that people choose to align with based on the consciousness they are experiencing.

When these are not the primary views of God, the ego will simply deny God or see it as something vengeful to fear. It will take the position, "How can all these terrible things happen in the world? God must be angry or something mean." This view is the exact opposite of its true nature of love. The ego holds on to this viewpoint to maintain its hold on the individual.

Finally at the last stance, the ego takes the viewpoint of indifference. It sees God as neither good nor bad, but it is unconcerned with it and has no particular interest in it. All of these views on God are false and nonbeneficial for our long-term growth as human and spirit beings.

Eventually, one will take a leap of faith maybe through a life experience or after exposure to truthful knowledge that delivers a clearer perspective on life. Faith is necessary to maintain the relationship between the human and the life energy we term as God. Without faith and belief in something beyond ourselves, we are limited in our outlooks on life and spiritual progress. With faith, consciousness is free to grow. Level of consciousness is based on the degree one feels separate from God. Feeling separate results in suffering. Feeling one with God results in peace.

As consciousness begins to align with truth and the ego loosens its grip, the God view becomes permitting and enabling. Consciousness begins to feel empowered and trusting of its newfound outlook on life. Individual consciousness continues to grow, and God is progressively seen as inspiring, merciful, and wise. It has infinite power that is creative, grateful, compassionate, and filled with knowledge and intelligence. Life is greatly fulfilling with these views on God because one becomes more aligned with truth and reality rather than falsehood and subjectivity.

As consciousness reaches the level of love, the God view becomes loving as its primary expression. Love turns into lovingness; consciousness becomes one with God's unconditional love. Beyond this God view remains a nondualistic expression of everlasting love, joy, and peace. Consciousness aligns itself with the ultimate truth of being one with love, joy, and peace.

Spirit vs. Ego

The game of life is an inner battle between spirit and ego. Let's say we have two remote controls within us that determine if we are aligned with spirit or ego. We have the power over the remote controls and constantly direct our next moves, choices, actions, and reactions.

The ego's and spirit's remote control are very different in their nature. The ego's remote control is dark; the spirit's remote control is light and luminescent. Both remote controls have buttons (like a video game controller or a TV remote), and they lay in front of us at all times. When we press the buttons (just like a normal controller), a corresponding response occurs. The ego always wants us to press the buttons on its remote quickly and sporadically and not think twice about it; the spirit presses its own buttons calmly and responsibly.

Inside our minds, the buttons are available, waiting to be pressed. We can see our thoughts and intentions as the power source that initiates or determines which buttons we press and which remote control we use. Each button we click causes an emotional response inside of us (like a character in a video game responds when we press the buttons on the game controller).

Right now, we are in the 3-D game of life, looking out as the character we chose at the start. When we chose this character, we were automatically forced to use both remotes (or so it seemed). The ego inside of us acts like the outside source that tries to control our moves and feelings in the game. It is like someone is always yelling at us, handing us the ego's remote, and telling us which buttons to press in order to change the way we feel to what it thinks is appropriate. We have become so used to this that we have been tricked into listening to the commands of the ego and using its dark remote that promote suffering within us.

The ego has a wide range of buttons on its remote that make us feel a variety of inner feelings. For example, the ego remote control looks like this:

- X button (fear)
- Triangle button (desire)
- Square button (anger)
- R1 button (guilt)
- R2 button (grief)
- L1 button (apathy)
- L2 button (shame)
- Select button (pride)

Notice that all the feelings that are brought on when we press the buttons on the ego's remote control are a form of suffering to different degrees. They don't make us feel good, and it is clear we should not be pressing these buttons and living under its control.

The moment we realize that we have an amazing spirit remote control with buttons that are a thousand times stronger and more fulfilling than the ego's, we can start pressing our own buttons and determining our own feelings and experiences. The spirit's remote control looks like this:

- C button (courage/affirmation)
- N button (neutrality/trust)
- W button (willingness/optimism)
- A button (acceptance/forgiveness)
- R button (reason/understanding)
- L button (love/reverence)
- M button (joy/serenity)
- I button (peace/bliss)

All the above buttons create positive inner experiences and are clear they are self-rewarding. If you are experiencing any of the feelings brought on by one of the ego's buttons, surrender your hold on the button, and replace it by pressing one of the inner spirit's buttons.

Think about it. The ego doesn't even have hands. It is not capable of clicking the buttons on its remote control. It is like a voice that never really has any power to do anything. Its only power is tricking us into pressing the buttons it wants us to push. The ego only has a silly remote control. It uses our hands (our minds and thoughts) and our power to press its buttons. So why are we clicking the ego's buttons in the first place?

The ego has one big trick up its sleeve. It tells us that it is the "inner me" that we identify with as self, and it disguises itself behind us. Because it has camouflaged itself as us since the beginning of our lives, it can walk us through why we should press its buttons and when we should push them. We believe it because we think it is us, and we go along holding its controller, clicking its buttons, and feeling the resulting different degrees of inner suffering and unpleasant feelings.

Take your hand (your mind) off the ego's buttons. Now pick up the ego's remote control and throw it away. You don't need it anymore. Now pick up your spirit's remote control (realign the mind with spirit) and notice it is singing with pleasure as it reassures you everything will be okay. All that is left to do is have fun clicking the all-new, rewarding buttons (feelings) at your disposal. Live your life with this new remote control, and enjoy the freedom it grants your inner experience.

Orange Analogy

Let's say you were an orange and you knew you were an orange. What part of the orange would you want to be? Do you want to be the hard and bitter outer peel or the sweet and enjoyable inner fruit? So what would you want to be? The fruit!

Now let us look at this in terms of our lives. We too have an outer peel and an inner sweet fruit. We can refer to the ego as the outer peel, which is cold and bitter. The spirit, as the inner fruit, is joyful and happy. The inner fruit (spirit) is always there, but the majority of the world is identifying with their outer peel (ego). Why? Ignorance and mis-identification with the surface of life that we sometimes lose touch with the best part of our being.

When eating an orange, we throw away the bitter peel to get to the sweet fruit because it is better and more enjoyable. We don't want to experience bitterness. We want to have a pleasurable experience. It should be just as obvious to acknowledge that a human being is the same way. We too have to peel away the ego to experience the glory of the spirit. If you tap into your inner fruit of joy, life will become a pleasurable experience.

The Jungle of Consciousness

With such a wide variety of human beings identifying at different levels of consciousness, we can see the world as like the jungle of consciousness. Just like in the Amazon rain forest where everything is living together and surviving in different ways, it is the same with us. The earth is a place where all consciousness levels are mixed together on the journey through life, living together, working together, and trying to relate with one another. This is why a lot of confusion and frustration takes place. Everyone sees and experiences the world a little different and expects and assumes others to see the world the same way as him or her. People don't understand how and why people are the way they are. "How can people be so ignorant? How can people be so mean?" These are common concerns. Learning the nature of consciousness helps us understand the reasoning behind people's actions. When the nature of consciousness is understood, forgiveness is an automatic consequence of that comprehension.

Different consciousness levels have dissimilar ways of expressing. For example, the consciousness level of acceptance handles things very differently than the consciousness level of fear. Let's just say one person was aligned with fear consciousness, and another was aligned with acceptance. Both are sitting on the couch and watching the news. The news is showing an ongoing war in a country, and people are rebelling against their leader in hopes of changing the democracy of the country. The TV shows riots and chaos as this is taking place.

The person aligned with fear consciousness will be watching this and be overwhelmed with fearful thoughts. He or she will be thinking, "What if this or that happens?" thinking the world is a scary place to live. Anxiety overwhelms him or her. He or she will experience feelings as if they are a part of what is going on in the news. Even when the news story is over, he or she may remain dwelling on the fearful thoughts.

On the other hand, the person aligned with the consciousness level of acceptance will be watching from a nonpersonal point of view and not investing himself or herself in the problem. He or she may be concerned with what is going on in the other country and have deep compassion for the people but accepting of the fact that it is out of his or her control with the awareness that changing his or her inner feeling will not fix the problem. He or she will move on with his or her life when the news story is done.

The relationship with consciousness is the ultimate factor that determines the expression of one's feelings and experience of one's life. These mixing levels of consciousness all in one place can create turbulence and disturbances amongst the people. People who have no respect for themselves have no respect for others and will project this onto others. People who do have respect for themselves don't understand how someone else could do something so rude to another human being. It is because of the alignment with consciousness. It accounts for everything.

Undoubtedly, people in this world say and do things that are sometimes impossible to understand. When someone directs something extreme toward you, understand that it is impersonal. The consciousness level that directs negativity toward you is incapable of knowing or doing better because they don't know another way in that moment. They are sensitive beings that are suffering inside and need a way to let it out. It is their way of survival. Have compassion for individuals who seem negative in day-to-day life because they are lost and unsure how to deal with this life. Never take things personal because, the moment we do, the victim mentality arises, and all of a sudden, we feel there is reason to blame. We go over and over in our minds how bad someone is and get thrown into a bunch of negative inner feelings.

Instead, maintain compassion for all beings. The energy field of compassion will serve your well-being.

Awakening a Peaceful Perspective

Don't let perceived worldly problems become your problems by reacting to them. Zoom out from the issues, and see life as a spiritual playground full of necessary tests. Life has to be this way for our spiritual growth. Everything happens for reasons far greater than our understanding. The ongoing of life don't have to be classified as right and wrong.

Let the jungle of life pan out how it is supposed to without our constant interrupting and inner commenting. It is easier to live this way. We become free from the jungle and can finally experience life in peace.

Think of yourself as a nonjudgmental viewpoint. Let's say you were watching the world and all of its activities from above and looking down at earth as a nonactive participant. You see the happenings of life have to be the way they are for the growth of the participants.

With this perspective, it would be ridiculous to judge and invest yourself in the specifics of everything going on. It is just as ridiculous now as we live our lives on earth. Instead, observe from a nonlocal viewpoint, love the process of life unfolding, and simply take joy in the fact you are aware of life in the first place.

Nonjudgment

Judgment is not possible when we understand the nature of consciousness and karma. When we judge, we are zoomed into the movie of life too much to the extent we are reacting to every little thing. When we zoom out, we see karma is merely playing out as it should and has to. Judging something or someone because you think it is worse than something else is coming from the wrong perspective. Consciousness is all equal and should be treated that way. People are merely aligned with different energy fields progressing through the evolution of life.

We can compare judging and forming categories about people to liking one piece of grass better because it is on a hill and not liking another because it is in the valley. Both are grass. At this level of understanding, it is the same as liking one person and then loathing another. They are both consciousness but just at different positions. All is to be accepted and loved equally.

Staying with the grass analogy, it can be viewed as our outgoing love can be seen as the nutritious water that helps the grass grow. We are the watering cans with control where our water (love) goes. If we only watered the grass on the hill and then went and stomped all over the grass in the valley, not enough water would be getting to the grass in the valley for it to grow.

We can compare stomping on the grass to judging. It does no good. Instead, we love all beings and water all the grass. When we live in this perspective, everything is beautiful and perfect and given equal opportunity to sprout to its full potential.

Spiritual Family

The current perspective is that everyone is divided and separate from one another to great extents. Countries, cultures, religions, races, and families are divided. We feel separate from one another, and where separation occurs as two opposites, conflict and problems arise.

We live in a world where the common belief is, if they aren't in your immediate family or close circle of friends, you are not obligated to care and love them the same as you would your own family. This is how the majority of the world's population lives. Why do we look at random people in day-to-day life and judge them as if they are different from us? When did this belief system become dominant among the masses?

If we look at a wolf pack, it has the exact same mentality. The wolves in the same pack work with each other and help one another survive. The wolf pack attacks and scorns any other group of wolves without hesitation as if they are enemies and seperate. Why did human beings adopt characteristics of a wolf pack? Are we not more evolved than this?

We need a new perspective, one more aligned with truth. This new point of view can bring harmony and unity to the world. It starts with each individual changing his or her way of perceiving one another one by one so it can become a movement in this new era.

From a spiritual perspective, we are the family of life, one big clan of spirits living in the physical world. As spirit beings, we come from the same source. We were all together at the beginning, and we will always remain collected. So-called random people you see in day-to-day life are actually your spiritual brothers and sisters on the journey through life. We can see the earth as the nurturing mother. We can see God as the unconditionally loving father. This accounts for terms like Mother Earth and Father of Grace.

Our mission is to help each other feel safe and find a sense of inner peace. We do this by becoming kind, compassionate, and loving above all else. As children united in the family, we are meant to love one another unconditionally and continue to grow to become like our Father. It is our goal and purpose and the reason why we are here right now, to make the world a better place and spread your kindness (positive, healing, and loving energy) for everyone in our family (including yourself). We should do this for three reasons:

1. It is why we came to earth, our purpose in life.
2. It helps our families become free from negativity.
3. We get to feel inner lovingness instead of suffering.

Yes, our spiritual brothers and sisters can make us angry and upset sometimes because of the things they do and say, but this is normal. Anyone who has a sibling in his or her immediate family knows fights and disagreement can sometimes happen. Bickering can take place, and grudges are held. But after all is said and done, we still love our siblings because it is our brothers or sisters. They are family, and the love holds the bond together. This is the same for all spiritual beings. We respect, care, and love them no matter what because, in the end, they are our greater family. All are just trying to do the best they can with what they know on their journey through life. We can appreciate the innocence in everyone with this new perspective.

The spirit is a giver. Committing your life to realign with your inner spirit means to pursue the path of the heart. Life becomes easier to handle, more fulfilling, exciting, peaceful, and enjoyable when lived in the spirit.

Father of Life

We have the best Father in the world:

- one that created us and asked nothing of us but to enjoy the experience of life
- one that gave us a spirit with everlasting life
- one that believes in us and knows our unlimited potentials

- one that creates beauty just for us to enjoy
- one that is patient and never disappointed or frustrated
- one that forgives us no matter our past faults
- one that sends angels to protect and guide us
- one that has loved us and will love us forever
- one that is always by our sides through the journey of life

Our Father is everything we wanted it to be and beyond. You get to the point where you admire, respect, appreciate, and love the Father and Creator of Life so much that you will do anything to be with this divine energy. So the journey to God begins. It starts within and grows beyond.

Nothing will stand in the way of living with the Father and Creator of Life. Nothing. All temptations, distractions, and attachments are surrendered for something far greater than anything in the physical. When the limitations are removed, the Father's presence awakens within, and the love, joy, and peace of being with this infinite energy overwhelm the experience of all moments.

People expect everyone in the world to be perfect and get frustrated and disappointed when the people do not meet their expectations and needs. We expect everyone to be like the Father/God when earth is the school to learn to become like the nature of God. You can expect God to be everything you expect others to be, perfect. God will surpass all expectations and needs, and that is an understatement. It is beyond words and needs.

On the path, one will realize he or she has been looking for God all along, but only he or she has been looking in the wrong place. Look within where the Father of Life is residing in you. The hand of God is always open with its palm extended to you to grab onto when one is ready.

CHAPTER 5

UNDERLYING BEHAVIOR

This section is included in the book to illustrate the restricting behaviors we consciously and unconsciously have that limit the experience of inner peace in day-to-day life.

Inner Challenges

Along the path to finding inner contentment, internal challenges face us. The goal is to have a self-sustained, enjoyable life experience that never wavers. Internal challenges block this very possible and ever-present experience of inner peace. These challenges are a combination of conscious and subconscious belief systems and positional viewpoints that justify underlying behavior that is not aligned with the overall goal to live in peace.

We face inner challenges on a daily basis in the form of self-judgment, appraisal of others, fears and worry, and any form of inner rationalization for holding onto negativity. If we retain any type of negativity such as shame, guilt, resentment, grudges, never-ending desire, fear, and so on, it is impossible to experience inner contentment because the negative qualities override the underlying peaceful experience of existence.

To the seeker of truth who has genuinely looked within himself or herself to see what is taking place, it becomes blatantly obvious we ourselves are the power source that initiates what is going on in our minds. We determine the inner experience. External factors can play an influential part, but when all is said and done, we are the determining factor with ultimate choice of how we want to express ourselves. Each individual chooses what he or she sees as important enough to him or her to hold onto it as an inner reality.

False-based underlying behavior can be a major hindrance to one's ability to be happy. If the goal is to sincerely find peace from inner suffering, we become honest with ourselves and take responsibility for what is going on inside of us. If we don't take responsibility, the mind will give someone to blame, some reason to be mad, upset, unhappy with the results of a specific outcome, judgmental about what is going on, and fearful about the future. And it will never end.

To speed up the process of living a joy-fulfilled life, we put our underlying behaviors in the spotlight. During this time of inner reflection, imagine a box that is labeled "Inner Behaviors That Hurt Me." Think about what you can do for yourself to make your life experience better. Look at your behaviors from a self-honest point of view. When the negative inner behavior is showcased to ourselves, we ask, "What is my benefit for holding onto this way of thinking?" If you have agreed with yourself that there is no benefit to you, mentally place it into the box. Look deep within yourself until you have found all the undesirable qualities you have agreed are not worth holding onto anymore. Place them all in the box, and seal it shut so it is inaccessible to you. Now visualize in your imagination that you are standing on the top of a mountain, holding the box that is labeled "Inner Behaviors That Hurt Me." When you are ready, throw the box off the cliff, and watch it fall until it is so far away that it drifts out of sight. This is a great exercise for freeing oneself from the restricting qualities of the false self. It can be done anytime a behavior in oneself needs surrendered.

The final step is to now imagine another box with a lid on it that is labeled "My Happy Spirit." Open the lid, and keep it ajar. Your inner spirit is now free to express its excitement, joy, and fearless lighthearted nature.

Self-Pressure

Everyone has witnessed or experienced the negative effects of bullying, whether it was as a child or an adult. Bullies put pressure on people and force them to do things they don't want to do. No one likes bullies, and most tend to avoid people with bully mentalities and forceful personalities. It's easy to understand why. They are no fun to be around and drain our positive energies. Now here is an interesting question. Who is the biggest bully in your life?

Instantly, you might think it's a silly question. You might think, "I don't have a bully." But there is an awakening realization. One very present bully affects each of our lives, our own minds. That's right. Our own minds bully us. Let's think about it. Our minds make us experience negativity in the form of shame, guilt, grief, anger, fear, and so forth, the very same emotions a typical bully can make someone feel.

We have been bullied our entire lives. Every time we experienced negativity and inner suffering, our own thoughts bullied us. Because we have been bullied for so long and are so used to it, we have adapted to it and accepted its negative presence in our lives. Every time we experience inner negativity, we are allowing ourselves to be bullied.

Our inner bullies have a way of putting pressure on us. Throughout the day, they can put us down, call us and other people names, create problems, judge, discriminate, justify negativity, and project negativity onto others. When we align ourselves with our inner bullies and listen to what they have to say, we force ourselves to endure the resulting suffering. The pressures we put on ourselves becomes overwhelming and almost too much bear. We live our lives under our inner created restrictions and limitations. The more forms of inner problems we experience, the more evident it is that our inner bullies are controlling our lives.

By putting pressure on ourselves for every little thing, it feels like there are tons of problems in our lives. Self-pressure equals inner problems. Self-pressure does not lead to happiness or constructive problem solving. Surrender it. It only adds to the confusion of life. We don't need to pressure ourselves to be a certain weight, look or act a certain way, or be something we are not. Embrace who you are. Let yourself shine to your fullest without the pressures of the mind speaking negativity. One easy rule to remember is to ignore everything that tells you not to be happy in each moment. They are all illusions.

It is time to enjoy and love ourselves instead of constantly judging and pressuring ourselves. Love the new you that arises from the knowledge that the real you (spirit) and the inner bully (the ego mind) are very different. The real you is already complete and happy. Identify with the real you, and experience your true nature of being perfectly perfect.

Seeking Gain

Life is lived in the form of seeking. Your spirit-seeking knowledge brought you to this book. The constant seeking for something more or better keeps most people going. To seek something better and more fulfilling in our lives is quite natural.

However, during this process of seeking something better, we see what other people have and how glamorous and satisfying their lives seem. We can become jealous and feel we deserve better, too. The problem arises when we replace seeking betterment with searching for gain. When we start to look for gain in any sort of way, we create the inner feeling of being in lack of. Because we seek to gain something, we tell our minds that we are lacking that one item and it is not available to us until sometime in the future. Believing we lack is the source of our unhappiness. The energy field of desire develops a never-ending craving to fill that desire. In this state of mind, it is impossible to reach the condition of inner peace and contentment in the present moment because, in the back of the mind, that inner voice says something better is somewhere out there.

When we seek to gain something, we create an outgoing forceful energy on whatever we are looking for. This pushes it farther out of our reach like a repelling magnet. Every time we subconsciously or consciously seek to gain something, we make it harder for ourselves to actually get it. It is like when we seek to gain that we create universal restrictions. We place limitations and obstacles in front of the very thing or aspect we seek. When the gain aspect of seeking is surrendered, a clear path opens between us and the thing we seek. Like magnets, they are then attracted together.

There is no need to worry when we hear "Seeking to gain is wrong" because it is actually quite normal. The negativity associated with it can be resolved in an instant when we change our perceptions toward whatever we are seeking. We can change the forceful and repelling energy into a positive and attracting energy.

We can successfully attract what we seek in our lives with the law of attraction, which has been taught for a long time, but because of its simplicity, it is often misunderstood. We can achieve the law of attraction by imagining and visualizing in our minds whatever we seek and acting as if we already have it. When we imagine as if we already have whatever we are seeking and project it out into the universe without looking for gain, the universe will manifest it as if it were a reality when the time is right, if it is meant to be for the highest good.

The instant we remove the seeking for gain element in our minds and stop telling ourselves we are lacking something, we let the law of attraction take full effect in our lives. That which is held in the mind has a tendency to manifest. Simply hold in mind what you want to attract into your life.

To surrender looking to gain something, we can focus on what we already have and simply imagine what we are looking to attract into our lives as if we already have that as well. Imagining in the mind's eye as if it were a reality without seeking to gain is the secret to attracting your wishes into your life.

Focusing on the Negative

The experience of living in itself is better than we could ever imagined. But in order to see it as so, we have to zoom out from the inner problems. We can be too focused on what is not—what is not going on in our lives, what is not available to us, what is not possible for us, and what we do not have—that we fail to see all the great things available to us.

There are usually only a very few number of problems and negative aspects in our lives and billions of positives. Yet the mind is addicted to spending the majority of its time focusing on the negative what-nots and don't-haves. We experience what we focus on. When we focus on something that makes us happy, we feel good. Just as well when we focus on the perceived negative aspects of our lives, we feel worse.

Focusing on the negativities of our lives does not solve them. Somehow it feels like, when we think about something negative that is bothering us, we are figuring it out and fixing the problem. The opposite is true. Thinking negatively toward a problem actually prevents us from seeing the opportunities to solve it. When we focus on the negative, we are actually creating and elaborating the problem in our minds. The only way to really solve a problem is by accepting it for what it is and taking action to be a part of the solution. If problems don't even need an action-based solution, they should be treated as an illusion and surrendered immediately. When we discover that an inner problem is just a nonrewarding elaboration in the mind, it is no longer worth our time or energies.

In order to live a life that is free from negative suffering, problems, and never-ending craving for something more, we must surrender focusing on the what-nots and the don't-haves and instead focus on all the positive and wonderful aspects of our lives. For every negative, there are ten thousand positives. To attract the positive in our lives, we identify with all these affirmatives instead of the one negative. We will find freedom in this new positive identification. Positive thoughts will override our consciousness and create affirmative, everlasting experiences in our lives.

Zooming Out of a Perception Exercise

You can use this exercise when something is bothering you and you are finding it hard to get over it.

Imagine you are looking at a round globe and zoomed in on a specific point in a particular area. Now imagine slowly panning back and zooming out from that point. Notice the expansion of perception. First, you see more details and sections of the globe, and as you continue to zoom out, you see how each section and piece of the puzzle plays an equal part in the greater picture. When you are zoomed all the way out, you realize there was no reason to limit your perception to one specific point when you had the choice to see the entire beauty of the globe.

Now do the same exercise with the negative aspects of your life that have been bothering you. Think of the specific problem or worry, and slowly zoom out from that particular point in your mind. Move away from that perception, and watch it fade away into the greater picture of living right now. When we zoom out of specific worries in our minds, we become free from them.

It is like we are focused right on the stressor in our minds, and we therefore experience that worry or problem. We can accomplish the process of zooming out of our inner worries and negative perceptions via the following steps:

1. Bring the perceived worry or problem to the surface of your mind.
2. Examine the perceived negative aspects of the problem.
3. Remove yourself from center of the issue.
4. Zoom out and focus on the greater picture.
5. Experience life in this very moment.

Following these five steps can take us from focusing on a specific negative perception or problem in our minds and bring us back to concentrate on experiencing the happenings of right now. Zoom out of the mind and into the now.

Nonresistance

When something is really bothering us in the world or our thoughts, what is the first response? Is it to react? How do we react? Is it with resistance? The term "resistance" is defined as refusal to accept or comply with something.

Has this ever happened to you? You are having a good day, and all of a sudden, something takes place that disrupts your well-being. You go from being happy to angry, upset, sad, and various other draining emotions. This takes place because we refuse to accept what took place. This is a form of resistance. By refusing to accept something for what it is or what happened, an outgoing energy is released from us that is trying to fight back or change what is taking place. The energy goes out into the world, notices the resistance point we are focusing on, and brings it back to us to create an inner negative experience directly related to that which we are resisting. We react to whatever is bothering us by resisting it. But when we resist it, we experience it.

The vast majority of people feel they need to hold on to the problems of the world or challenging thoughts and fears in their minds because, by continuing to go over them, they are somehow solving the issues and taking a stance for what is right.

The fact is this continued thought process puts us into a negative-thinking spiral. It is like we create a circle of adverse energy in our minds, and it keeps going around and around and around, and we don't know how to stop it. There is a way to break the circle of negativity so we don't have to experience it. It's called nonresistance.

The act of nonresistance is the process of inviting the issue. As weird as this may sound, in order to eliminate the perceived problems and fears in our minds, we need to do the exact opposite of what we would normally think to do. We think inviting the problem or fear would cause it to intensify, and we think resisting it will help solve or stop it. The opposite is true. That which you don't want to experience causes you to resist it, which enfolding it brings it to the forefront of the inner experience. That which you resist, you experience.

When you don't want to have to experience something that is going on in your mind, invite it in and accept it. When we invite it with sincerity, it will begin to subside. Trick yourself and say, "I want to experience this," and then when you want to experience it, witness it disappear. The funny thing about the mind is that it won't let you experience what you want to. It does the opposite.

We can train ourselves into this opposite way of thinking. The act of nonresistance has the power in it to diminish our inner problems. When a problem arises in your mind, take the following steps:

1. Focus on the perceived problem, fear, and/or issue.
2. Invite it into your inner experience.
3. Ask to experience it and say, "I want to feel this."
4. Watch the mind do the opposite.

When you want to feel the fear or problem that is causing you suffering, your mind doesn't let you experience what you want to feel, so it all fades away. It sounds almost impossible to say, "I want to feel this fear" or "I want to feel this problem." You don't want to feel it. But this technique is proven to work. By not resisting anything that is taking place in your mind and actually taking one step beyond to meet the very thing that causes you anxiety, the stressor shies away and diminishes, it becomes shy in the spotlight. Same can be done with random never ending parade of thoughts. Stop for a moment and ask your mind to give you your next thought. Suprisingly the mind just might shut up for a second.

When we follow these simple steps with sincerity, our problems, fears, and suffering in the mind will begin to fade away. We can live a life of nonresistance and carry this attitude into all aspects of our lives. If something arises that we feel is wrong or don't like, we can accept it with nonresistance by following the steps above and notice that we don't have to experience it when we don't resist the negativity.

Judging vs. Wishing Better

There is no harm in admitting that most people are obsessed with judging. Actually, very few people can say with honesty that they have gone one entire day without a single judgment about themselves or someone else. Judgment in others is a reflection of what one judges in himself or herself. So if you don't like something in yourself, it is mirrored in the judgment of others. Self-acceptance helps in relinquishing outgoing forms of conclusions.

We may sometimes not even notice ourselves judging or condemning others because it is overshadowed by the reasoning we have built up in our minds that tells us it is okay to judge or think this way in this certain situation because we are right and the other person, position, and so forth is wrong. Because we think it is wrong or bad, under certain conditions, we feel we have the right to condemn, judge, and look down upon it.

In order to advance our inner growth, we give up all judgment, no matter the form. Reaching peace requires a life without judgment. Every time a verdict takes place, we give away some of our inner powers. By judging others, we show we are not yet fully comfortable with ourselves. Inner resolution arises when we get comfortable and complete enough in ourselves that we feel no need to judge others. Self-acceptance also makes people more comfortable to be around you. Remember, others are as comfortable with you as you are accepting of yourself.

Sometimes, people find it hard to stop their automatic, engrained judgments and negative reactions when exposed to something they disagree with. It may be beneficial to replace automatic judgments with "wishing better" thinking. When we catch ourselves thinking negative and judgmental thoughts, we should replace them with positive and "wishing better" thoughts. When we wish better for someone or something instead of judging, we feel the positive over the negative, and we spread power instead of force. It feels good to wish better for someone, and it feels bad to judge someone. That is all the proof we need to wish better instead of judge.

We can know that, every time we wish better for something or someone and think positive toward that thing or person, we are increasing their capacity to improve and heal, all the while equally increasing our own capacities to feel good. This is the power of a prayer and the reason why it can do the miraculous. It is said that we should live life like a prayer. This means we never waver from sending positive and uplifting intentions and remain in the prayer of life. When we live life like a prayer, we become a healing and uplifting energy.

We know it is more rewarding for ourselves not to judge, but now it becomes about how aware we are of our judgments and how willing we are to replace these verdicts with betterment (positive and uplifting) thoughts. When we consistently make this change, it soon becomes automatic and opens a new way of experiencing life where each moment gives us the opportunity to help the world and ourselves.

Once we come to terms with the reality that everything and everyone around us will never be exactly the way we want it to be, we can simply focus on being exactly the way we want ourselves to be. Certain people cannot help acting the way they do and being the way they are because they are living under the restraints of a specific energy field that they feel they have no control over. If we disagree with certain people, does it make sense to let their position in life disrupt your well-being? No, it is not worth the energy.

We don't have control how people are, but we do influence the way we see them and how we choose to express ourselves toward others. Depending on if we choose to judge or wish better upon others determines if we are maintaining our inner energies or letting something disrupt its natural flow.

Self-Programming

Sam doesn't feel good, and he doesn't know why. He tells himself he is willing to do anything to feel better and starts to think about how he can create a better inner feeling. He asks himself, "Where do I start? How do I start feeling better?"

Sam finds himself lost and looking for a way to just be happy, but he doesn't know how or where to start. This frustrates him. He searches for ways to feel better. Then he has an awakening realization. *Nothing can make me feel happy and content but myself because what I feel toward everything else determines the way I feel inside.* And with this new insight, Sam now has a starting point to create a new way of seeing and reacting to the world so he can enjoy a positive inner experience at every moment.

Sam starts by changing the way he feels toward himself. He realizes he has been in a love/hate relationship with himself his entire life. Sometimes, Sam likes Sam. Other times, Sam hates Sam. It was normal to go through the day and be critical of how he is as a person, judgmental about what he says and does and feel small and unworthy at times. He remodels his thoughts to be positive and constructive toward himself. Sam starts by staying aware in each moment and catching his thoughts that are directed at him. If they are not positive in nature, he surrenders them and replaces them with an "I am" statement such as "I am happy/lovable/confident" or any positive reinforcement statement that is appropriate at the time. After changing the way he views himself, it soon becomes normal for Sam to think positive about him. Negative thinking toward himself fades away, and he can finally truthfully say and believe, "I love myself." He has begun to renown his inner power, and he starts to feel a little bit better already.

Sam is now confident moving forward and continues by changing the way he feels toward the people around him. One by one, he surrenders all of his built-up opinions, judgments, and negative feelings toward the people in his life because, with these negative qualities of the mind, he knows it is impossible to feel better inside. When he has accepted this and realizes it is easier to have compassion than to judge and condemn, he transcends this negativity and moves on to the next step to finding inner contentment. With this new way of seeing and relating with people, he no longer has to feel the negative emotions that sprout from judging and forming opinions about others. Instead, a consistent, positive experience of compassion toward others replaces the negativity. His inner experience is no longer always changing from good to bad.

Sam moves on to changing the way he feels toward all other aspects in his life in which he has a negative opinion, view, or feeling about. Every one of these adverse perspectives causes him to feel worse inside when he thinks about them. He understands that the only way he is going to feel better is if he surrenders these negative positionalities. He reexamines the way he feels toward everything that makes him feel worse and changes how he sees them so it doesn't cause him internal stress. He finally feels in control and confident in his ability to change his outlook on life. With fixity of focus in each moment, Sam deliberately replaces negative perceptions with positive thinking and reprograms his mind to release positive and feel-good chemicals and endorphins. He starts to feel the inner happiness and contentment he has always sought. He realizes he had the power within him all along to change his inner experience.

His life continuous on, and Sam notices a great inner feeling arising. He is excited to take on each day. He has lots of energy to do whatever he needs to do and feels no resistance toward anything that is taking place. He feels refreshed and can now enjoy the experience of life. He has successfully freed himself from his negative self that caused the suffering and realigned with the positive person who was inside him all along.

Anyone can follow Sam's path to inner freedom. The reprogramming starts with making an agreement with us. We tell ourselves, "From this moment on, I will maintain only positive intentions because I deserve to feel good." When we maintain a positive way of being with fixity of focus, a content inner experience arises. The only noncontentment that is there in the first place was us saying something isn't right or should be better and so forth. It may sound cheesy to some, but for the people who try it out in their own lives, they will experience a change of well-being.

When you catch yourself in a negative thought pattern or perception for whatever reason, you know you are on the right path because you noticed yourself thinking that way. Now that you have caught yourself thinking negatively toward something, you have an inner awareness and opportunity to surrender that way of thinking in that moment.

Consciously and unconsciously, we are programming the way we feel. Our inner feelings are a result of our outer projections. When we change these from negative to positive, we feel the resulting inner rewards. It is simple, yet it can seem very difficult because we are so used to the negative automatic reactions that occur inside of us when we see or experience certain forces in the world. This is why self-awareness is so important. Without it, we begin to ride the wave of negative thoughts and subconsciously program ourselves into inner problems and suffering. With self-awareness, we can see the rising negative thought and choose not to attach to it, instead replacing it with a neutral or positive thought and intention. With continued focus, introspection, and a respect for ourselves, we can establish a growing inner peace and happiness in our consciousness.

Belief Systems

Whatever you believe in, you attract into your life. Belief has its own power because, when you believe in something, it becomes real in your life based on you believing in it. So even if someone has faith in something that isn't necessarily true, the fact he or she believes in it makes it true and real to his or her inner experience.

This is why people are so easily misled. The innocence of the human mind is unlike anything else in the universe. It is unable to tell truth from falsehood. So if something is glamorized and packaged nicely, the human mind is gullible and persuaded into believing it. When the mind adopts a new belief, it attracts whatever its conviction is into its life experience.

The majority of the population is running on some sort of false belief systems that have been instilled into the mind from a young age. Belief systems are passed down from family, friends, media and taught all over the place. Just about everywhere you look, someone is promoting his or her own belief systems and convincing others to follow along. A belief is like an advertisement that people listen to. "If it sounds convincing enough and goes with my way of life, I will believe in it." Isn't that how it goes?

The problem lies when people hold onto false belief systems that truth does not back. A false belief is a waste of energy and hinders one's inner freedom. You become invested into a belief system to such an extent that you carry it with confidence because of the fact that it yours. After a long period of time in believing something, it becomes a part of you, and even if it is not true, it seems very hard to let go because it feels like you would be losing a part of yourself. This is why beliefs are not the best way to go when trying to figure out life. They become distractions and elaborated perceptions in the mind in which the viewpoint on life is restricted and the perspective of reality is slanted.

We pick up our belief systems from one another. Another person told us, "This is the way it is." And we went along with it. That person got his or her belief system from another person passing it down. And it goes on forever.

Some people have acquired so many beliefs that they feel like they are living in a box, but they feel safe there. Each belief limits the perspective of reality a little bit. With a variety of belief systems working together, it can feel like you know everything, and one becomes overly confident with his or her views of life to the extent that he or she doesn't allow anything else to enter, even when it is real truth. He or she becomes increasingly confident with his or her beliefs until the point that he or she thinks he or she has figured it all out and there is nothing else to learn. And so nothing else is learned, and life becomes a continuous process of the same thing over and over. And he or she wonders why he or she is feeling good. Even the greatest teachers are primarily a dedicated student, and as they teach, they continue to be open to learn.

You need an open mind to be receptive to truth; you need exposure to truth to grow consciousness. Without hundreds of belief systems clouding your judgment and restricting your internal growth, you can start to experience truth rather than just believing in it.

Imagine for a second that you had absolutely no beliefs. You just were. What is left? Pure awareness, the state of peace people are trying to reach. This is not to say that you should not believe in anything. This section is included to illustrate the power of belief and the importance of an open mind and give guidance to not believe in every little thing you hear. Ask yourself, "What do I get out of believing in this?" If a belief only goes as far as a thought, it is not worth your investment. If you don't get anything out of it except a slanted perception of reality, it is not really worth holding onto.

This book is not here to make you believe in anything. It provides guidance and knowledge backed with truth so you can turn the knowledge into a verifiable experience so it doesn't need to be backed with belief. It becomes an experiential reality. When truth-based knowledge is put into practice, the freedom that is experienced within will be all the belief you need. That is why *Knowledge Is Freeing*.

A baby is happy because he or she hasn't been exposed to thousands of beliefs systems and invested in them to create a distorted version of life. He or she is just what he or she is and happy that he or she is. A baby is the closest thing to enlightenment because he or she is still pure and fully in the moment without altered beliefs that tells him or her that he or she has to be like this or that.

When it comes to believing in a higher energy like God, you don't need to believe in it. It is a knowingness, not a belief in the mind. Knowledge-based faith, to know based on its experiential reality. It is a reality, not a belief system.

Belief is something you hear, adopt, and accept as being true. An inner knowingness beyond a belief system can be termed as faith. To have faith means there is no underlying doubt because it is a reality. You don't have to believe in a reality because you know it exists based on experience. You know you have a hand, so you don't say, "I believe I have a hand." No, you know you have a hand without a doubt. Faith and knowingness of the reality of God is the same. You don't just believe in it. You know it exists because it is even more apparent than your hand. God is the awareness of life. You know you have cognizance, so you have an inner knowingness of its existence without the added cling-on of belief.

Truth is rooted in reality, and when you hear truth, there is no need to believe it or not because the inner freedom it brings is dominant over a secondary belief system. Only believe in that which you know from experience, and then it is not even called a belief. It is called a reality.

Integrity

In the past, people who lacked integrity lied to you. Life has never lied to you. Life is working with you and supporting you. Life is the ultimate role model. If you want to live truthfully in reality and aligned with life, one must have integrity. Integrity is honesty.

Be honest with yourself first and foremost, and then spread that attitude to others. Integrity is an internal consistency as a virtue. You become integrous for the sake of living in truth, not just because it is morally correct. You build a respect and relationship with truth.

Inner suffering, as in negative emotions such as apathy, guilt, anger, fear, shame, and others, are not forms of integrity. It is non-integrous to accept suffering as a way of being. No inner suffering is justifiable. If you introspectively examine when you are living in or how you are experiencing a negative emotion, you see it possibly stems from the fact you are trying to prove to yourself that you are right.

We try to prove to ourselves we are right, and there is a good enough reason to feel this way because something in the big, bad world did this or that. It comes down to how much we are willing to sacrifice and pay to be right. If you are willing to not be happy in order to get the satisfaction of being right and sticking with your belief systems that don't support your inner well-being, then happiness will always be something in the distant future that one hopes for. It goes, "Oh, well. Maybe tomorrow will be better." Tomorrow won't be better if today isn't better because the feeling of betterment has to come from you. After the light of truth reawakened her, Betty J. Eadie said, "We can create our own spiral of despair, or we can create a trampoline of happiness and attainment" (*Embraced by the Light*).

Be integrous with yourself to allow contentment and happiness to become more important than proving and convincing yourself that you are right and the world is wrong in some way or someone did you wrong. Chances are, you are right, and someone did do something that wasn't correct. When you let it control your well-being, you are letting whatever happen have power over you.

Self-integrity for the sake of well-being is the bridge between falsehood and truth. When you adopt integrity, you renounce the relationship with negativity and start to reclaim your power. As we acknowledge and let go of trying to prove to our inner selves that we are right and there is a justifiable reason for each negative feeling, suffering will fall away, and well-being will be free to arise.

CHAPTER 6

INNER FEELINGS

This chapter focuses on the inner feelings that free us from suffering. We have heard that the source of happiness comes from within. This section elaborates how to live in contentment and find happiness by establishing a new relationship with inner feelings.

Source of Inner Feelings

What is the source of inner feelings? At all times, almost everything we could possibly imagine is happening in this very moment. People are getting married. Others are skydiving, having an argument, eating supper, laughing at a joke, starting a new business, learning yoga, or thinking about penguins. You name it, it is taking place right now somewhere in this world.

Birth is a miracle, and happiness overwhelms individuals when they are a part of the experience. Do we feel full of happiness every second a baby is born and sad every second someone passes away? No, that is impossible. Our focus of attention is not on this in day-to-day life. This shows that not what is going on in the world determines if we are happy or sad. How we choose to invest ourselves in the ongoings and how we interpret what is going on determines the inner feeling that is experienced.

Again, everything we could imagine is taking place right now. If inner feelings were dependent on what was going on around us, waves of tragedy and joy would overwhelm us every second, and we would have no control over the matter. This is just not how it works. Anyone who looks at inner feelings from a clear perspective will realize we only experience that which we focus our attentions on. The change of focus of attention and an inner reaction to it bring on the change of inner feeling. An example can illustrate this:

> Duncan is a pilot who lives in a condo in Atlanta. Right now, he is working and in the process of flying a 747 airplane. He is focused on the safety of the passengers in the transportation from Atlanta to Chicago. He feels fine, and he focuses his attention on the duties of flying the airplane. Meanwhile back in Atlanta, his dog got into the garbage and made a mess on the floor in his condo. Because Duncan's focus of attention is on flying the airplane and not the dog's little incident, he experiences no change in his inner feeling. Hours pass, and Duncan finishes his flights. He is feeling great on his way home. When he gets home, he finds what the dog has done and gets upset.

Now here is where the focus of attention changed and a reaction took place that resulted in a change in Duncan's inner feelings. He went from feeling great to upset in just a moment. The reaction to something caused the change of feeling. If he were to simply clean up the mess and not have a reaction, nothing would have changed inside of him. Instead, he chose to react with anger, and this resulted in the feeling of being upset. While flying the plane, Duncan had no idea the dog was making a mess, and he didn't feel any change in emotion while it was actually taking place. This proves it is not what is going on in the world but what takes place inside of us that accounts for our changing feelings. It is not a cause and effect world.

It is all about what we choose to focus our attentions on and how we choose to react. The response determines the change of feelings we experience. The thing we are reacting to is actually irrelevant. How we perceive it determines if our reactions will be positive or negative. It will be an affirmative reaction if we perceive it to be good and negative if we see it to be bad. See diagram below:

(Situation occurs -> perceive as good or bad -> determines how we react -> results in the inner feeling)

While this automatic response was built into us since birth, it is beneficial to realize that everything just is the way it is and beyond our control in an external sense. Having a negative reaction, metallization, or comment about anything does no good for our well-being and creates inner feelings of suffering. The critical point is to change the way you perceive what is going on. If you previously thought something to be bad, replace it with the knowingness that it is less desirable but not worthy of a negative response from you.

From the diagram above, it is clear we actually have complete control over our inner feelings. By reexamining how we perceive what is going on, removing the falsehood reaction system that has been running our inner experiences, and becoming the lighthearted version of ourselves, we can be free from inner suffering and eventually full of inner happiness that is sustained from within. As you become more comfortable with maintaining a positive life experience, situations that unfold will have no negative effect on your inner happening. You can now shrug off that which once caused you stress and maybe even laugh.

Choices and Feelings

No matter what situation, big or small, a choice of how we react confronts us. For example, imagine you are driving to work. Someone cuts you off and slams on the brakes; this makes you slam on the brakes. You have two choices: choice A (ego self) and choice B (higher self).

In Choice A (ego self), the mind begins racing. You think, *That disrespectful driver! He just cut me off! Who does he think he is? People should learn how to drive. If you don't know how to drive, get off the road! People are crazy!* Now you pull up to person who cut you off and roll down the window. "Hey! Why don't you learn how to drive, moron? Go back and get some lessons!" You drive away.

If you went the route of choice A, now two people start out their days with a fresh batch of forceful energy. They get to work and try to suppress the energy, but as more force is sent toward them, it builds up within them throughout the day. Depending on the day they have, you can imagine how much forceful energy can build up inside them if they are not releasing it in some way.

We usually end up releasing it the negative energy built up inside of us and take it out on the people we love, as weird as that sounds. In the world, there is a responsibility to stay socially respectful. But at home, you are able to express yourself more freely. We get home from the day, and the negative energy of the day can be so built up that it can end up coming out toward the people we love. There is a way to stop this cycle of negative energy by taking a different approach to life that prevents the negative energy from building up inside of you in the first place. It is the process of surrendering it in the moment as it arises.

To break the cycle and the build-up of forceful energy and to stop releasing it back into the world, we can also approach life less seriously. We are all here to have a good time and feel joy and peace. It is fruitful to live lightheartedly. It is exciting to witness the change of perception. What once caused us anger can now bring contentment to our lives and make us laugh.

In Choice B (higher self), someone drives in front of you and puts on the brakes. First, the higher self may not even care the person cut him or her off or may not see it as a bad thing. The higher self might think, *Fine with me. I am in no rush to get to work anyway.* When someone cuts off another person, it probably slows that person down by around seven seconds. While the ego self feels the need to get mad about those seven seconds as if someone took them from it, the higher self is more focused on experiencing the positive in each moment and not looking for something to cling to that would cause potential negativity.

Or maybe when you are cut off, the instant thought arises, *He shouldn't have cut me off.* But then, the higher self catches the thought and tames it with, *Of course I don't want to be cut off.* Laugh at the situation and find humor in everyday occurances. The higher self can find it quite enjoyable to watch a new world unfold in which we do not have to experience negativity.

It is important to remember that, when something happens, like a car cutting you off, you instantly have the decision to replace the automatic negative reaction with a positive or neutral feeling that diffuses the adverse energy in that instant so you don't have to experience it. You can use any positive feeling to replace it. For example, if the car cuts you off, you could respond with the following positive responses:

- Forgive him or her, for he or she could be late for work and didn't see you there. Maybe he or she has to go the bathroom and isn't thinking clearly!

- Accept he or she did what he or she did because it didn't really affect anything at all. See it as impersonal and not worth your emotional investment.
- Have compassion for the individual, for he or she obviously has his or her own issues.
- Be happy for being able to experience life and all its bonuses like driving. Getting cut off isn't worth removing the happiness.
- Love the person who cut you off, and experience this emotion instead of anger and frustration. It is possible.

Whatever thoughts and feelings you choose, you get to experience that feeling instead of being upset, and instantly, the negative energy diminishes, and we don't have to carry it with us. As each potential problem in which a negative reaction may have seemed appropriate arises throughout the day, surrender it as it arises and use humor to diffuse the negative response.

The day will become better because, when we change how we see and react to the world, we get to feel that inner change inside of us. The saying, "When you change, the world changes," applies here. When no negativity is built up inside of us and we stop sending it out, our lives automatically becomes more peaceful. Dr. Wayne Dyer, the very well-known self-help teacher said in a live presentation, "If you change the way you look at things, the things you look at change."

So let's break it down even further to carry this way of thinking to all aspects of life. In every situation, we have a choice. The content of the situation doesn't matter. The choices always remain the same, starting from the negative and self-detrimental (forceful) to the positive and self-healing (power).

Bam! The situation occurs, and it is time to decide what level of consciousness we want to attach to in that very moment. Whichever level we attach to will determine the resulting emotion without exception. The choices and resulting negative emotions are as follows:

- If we choose shame, we feel humiliated.
- If we choose guilt, we feel blame.
- If we choose apathy, we feel despair.
- If we choose grief, we feel regret.
- If we choose fear, we feel anxiety.
- If we choose desire, we feel craving.
- If we choose anger, we feel hate.
- If we choose pride, we feel scorn.

By choosing any of the above reactions, we will create a negative feeling in ourselves. On the other hand, choosing one of the following responses will create a neutral or positive feeling no matter the situation:

- If we choose courage, we feel affirmation.
- If we choose neutrality, we feel trust.
- If we choose willingness, we feel optimistic.
- If we choose acceptance, we feel forgiveness.
- If we choose reason, we feel understanding.
- If we choose love, we feel reverence.

The illusion that we must restrict these choices depending on circumstances and outcomes is just that, trickery. We can choose to attach to any of these emotions every single second of our lives. We can outline the negative emotions one can attach to based on his or her inner perception toward the situation. For example, Jenna is fired from her job. Here are the potential negative reactions that can sprout based on her perception toward the situation:

- She can feel shame and humiliation for being fired and feel like she is "no good."
- She can blame someone else for getting fired but subconsciously feel guilty.
- She can feel apathetic, worthless, and sorry for herself to the point that she can't apply for another job.
- She can go back into her mind, regret something she did, and feel grief for what she seemed to have caused herself to lose.
- She can feel anxious and fearful about the situation of losing her job, not having enough money for the future, not being able to pay the bills, not being able to find another job, and so forth. She can feel a whole collection of fears sprouting from one fear.
- She can crave revenge and desire to get back at the boss who fired her.
- She can feel hate for the boss who fired her and have anger toward him or her.
- Pride can fill her, and she takes the position that she was too good for that job anyway.

The scary part with negative emotions is that they are interlinked with one another. So once you attach to one feeling, a bunch of others can sprout and become the center of your attention. On the other hand, here are the positive reactions Jenna can choose to attach to and experience the resulting positive inner feeling:

- She can feel courage to keep moving forward, let the past be the past, and move on.

- She can trust that everything will be okay and begin searching for a new job with no worries or stresses keeping her from making the right decisions. She doesn't necessarily feel good about the whole situation, but she doesn't feel bad either. She feels neutral.
- She can feel optimistic about the whole situation and be willing to let everything turn out the way it does. She can be hopeful and inspired to find a better, more rewarding job.
- She can forgive her boss for firing her and have complete acceptance for the situation.
- She can have understanding for the entire way the situation panned out. She can examine all sides of the perceived problem, know exactly why she was fired, and understand the reasoning behind the boss's actions. This is where she uses her intelligence rather than her emotions.

All of these positive emotions give us power rather than drain us. If we start attaching to the feelings of optimism, forgiveness, and understanding in all aspects of life, our lives become less stressful, and situations become more understandable and enjoyable.

Tapping into Inner Joy

You have probably heard before that all joy comes from within. But how do you spark it so it is an experiential reality? First, stop pursing it. Stop trying to find happiness and joy, and become it instead.

When you think something is important and then you get it, some joy fills you. Let's do an innocent example to illustrate this. Kim is four years old, and it is very important to her that she gets the bright pink bike with the white basket on the front. For her birthday, her parents buy her the new bike and tell her to come to the backyard for a surprise. The moment she sees the bike, excitement and delight overwhelms Kim. She runs to the bike, and her parents smile at one another as she joyfully jumps on the bike. With joy-filled eyes, she says, "Mommy, push me! Push me!"

Now, let's go back and take a different approach. Let's say Kim wasn't that into bikes this time. She is more of a girly girl, and jewelry is more important to her. She asks her parents to get her a sparkling pearl necklace that she saw in the store. She really likes the necklace and hopes she gets it for her birthday. When her birthday comes around, her parents tell her to go to the backyard for a surprise. She walks into the backyard and sees a pink bike with a big white basket. Kim instantly breaks down into tears and yells, "I don't like bikes! I wanted the pearl necklace!" She runs back inside the house in frustration. The difference in the reaction from joy to disappointment was the transformation in what Kim saw as important to her. This is the same with all of us.

When we think something is important, our elaborated perceptions of its importance makes it significant to us. When we get whatever we think is important, we feel joy. So in order to tap into inner joy, we change what we perceive as important to us.

Here is another quick example to show that you are the joy that comes from within. Let's say you bought a lottery ticket, went home, and read the winning numbers. And they all match up with your ticket numbers. Instantly, an overwhelming sense of joy rises over you. You do the million-dollar happy dance and feel uncontrollably happy. This feeling in that instant of realizing you won was brought on because all else was surrendered other than that of pure joy in that moment. Where did the feeling come from? No one injected happiness into you to have that experience. It solely came from within because something inside of you said it was appropriate to align with it in that instant. You became that joy and therefore got to experience it. What if that joy is always waiting for us to align with? What if we don't need anything to happen for us to feel inner joy?

Joy is an automatic experience when nothing is in its way. We are joyful beings with layers of other feelings dominating its presence. The source of joy is our lives. In order to experience it, we become it. How?

Don't do anything. Life is going perfectly according to plan. We can't do anything to force joy. We can surrender that which holds it back. You only have to do the best you can. Make each moment of your existence the most important thing to you. Realize your very existence is the most significant thing of all. Bypass putting importance on something out there, and turn it around to here and now. Let the inner gratitude of existing override all other feelings. Say, "I am happy to be alive," and believe it in your heart. If you live truthfully from within, joy will arise on its own accord when all that is standing in its way is surrendered.

Instant Joy

For the people looking for a way to experience instant joy, there is a way to do it. Are you ready? Laugh! It's no secret that laughing feels good. A nice long laugh lifts your spirits. The ability to even laugh is quite unique and remarkable. A human is the only living thing on the earth that can laugh. Animals can't do it although it would be funny if they could. Imagine seeing a cow laugh.

We should take advantage of the gift of laughter for it is great in its instantaneous results in creating an uplifted feeling. Use it to your full potential. Laugh any chance you get because it releases feel-good chemicals in the brain. People flock to comedy shows because they want to catch a buzz. A comedian's job is to basically loosen people up and make them feel good with jokes that stimulate laughter. In day-to-day life, we sometimes get caught up in the stresses of work and tend to take life too seriously and withhold our laughter. Being lighthearted opens ourselves up for more opportunities to laugh with the movie of life.

Tune yourself into life from your inner comedy channel. It is less stressful and more enjoyable that way. The things people do are hilarious when they are not harming others. Most people can't see this because they are tuned into the super serious channel and their inner TV burdens them. Situations and experiences are seen as personal and opportunities for judgment.

When life is understood for what it is and the ego characteristics in our mind are surrendered enough to take oneself less seriously, humor can be found anywhere. Life is one big comedy when viewed from the right channel. Laugh with the movie of life. No one said we have to play a dramatic character.

Happiness

To be happy for a few moments and to live in the state of happiness are two different things. Happiness is a consequence of the progression of consciousness, not an emotion. Happiness is a way of consciousness expressing itself with its awakened understanding of reality. It is more fruitful to focus one's attention on growing consciousness rather than forcing oneself to be happy.

If you want to experience real happiness, live with yourself in peace. Live the contemplative lifestyle that doesn't waver from existing in truthfulness. Surrender being the broadcaster of life and become the happy witness and observer.

Just like if you were driving a car and didn't know exactly how to get where you were going, first program the GPS to point to where you want to go. So in this case, we are en route to happiness. Enter it into your inner GPS, and begin the journey. As you start on the road, you may notice some obstacles are blocking you from getting there. Notice the roadblocks, and find a way to get them out of your path (surrender them) so you can continue forward on this exciting journey.

When all the roadblocks are removed, one effortlessly finds his or her way to the destination. It is like a helium-filled balloon with a bunch of strings of different lengths tied to the inflatable that keep it from floating freely. One by one, as each string is cut, the balloon goes higher and higher until the last string is finally cut and the object is free to float effortlessly into the sky. The balloon finds happiness in its new freedom. That's just it. Happiness comes from being free of limiting and restricting behavior that causes suffering. One is truly free to be happy when he or she has become a perfect reflection of life.

You don't have to have an external reason to be happy to release your inner happiness. As an exercise, simply at any random time, burst into a sense of joy and overwhelm yourself with extreme happiness. Do this as a practice to reprogram happiness. Right now, the majority of the population is living the illusion that something good has to happen for us to release a sense of being happy. Why do we wait for something?

Burst into happiness for no reason at all. Maintain it with consistency. We release happiness so we can be happy. Is that a good enough reason? After all, it is what everyone says they want.

Compassion

Compassion is a necessary component in the process of finding inner freedom. Dalai Lama, an inspirational teacher who has spent his life teaching love and compassion, once said, "One can overcome the forces of negative emotions, like anger and hatred, by cultivating their counterforces, like love and compassion."

Compassion is one of the key ingredients in our abilities to survive together in this world. It brings people together despite faults and differences. Let's imagine a world where compassion did not exist. People would not be able to relate with one another, and everyone would end up being enemies. The workplace would be a very uncomfortable place to work in with hateful energy flying around the room from person to person. Anything someone did that another person did not agree with would be considered terrible with no further thought process of why the person did what he or she did and what made him or her do it.

Compassion is the bridge that lets us see people in a different perspective so that what we witness in the world is not just coming from our judgmental single points of view. We put ourselves in someone else's shoes so we don't automatically go off in anger and hatred when we see wrong behavior. Compassion is another form of spiritual vision that, when initiated, shows the reasoning behind people's actions and their way of being. It helps us understand that people are innately innocent. Everyone is just being the best version of himself or herself that he or she can be in each moment. When living in compassion, this is evidently clear.

Almost everyone at his or her core is innocent and sensitive. You may be surprised to know that person who presents himself or herself to the public as the prideful and confident being is usually the most sensitive. His or her personality protects himself or herself. The public version of someone is usually the bulked-up version of the individual. It feels the need to build itself up because it sees a harsh world and doesn't want to be squashed like a bug. Some overcompensate this fear of humiliation, social disapproval, belittlement, and not being acknowledged by others by taking the approach of being cold and less caring. They generally have the "I don't care" attitude. This type of person usually goes on the attacking side of social situations that can come off as rude and ignorant mainly because he or she fears being the one getting judged on the other side. His or her current outlook on life makes him or her too sensitive to handle negativity directed at him or her so he so she subconsciously do the completely opposite in hopes of not being put in a situation he or she doesn't want to be in.

When we understand this, we can sprout compassion for all people. Individuals who seem to cause social turbulence need the most support. They do not need to be judged. When they are reviewed and ridiculed, they just elaborate their behavior and get more cold and non-caring.

Try to keep an open point of view with people. We never know what someone is going through in his or her life, and people sometimes simply need to vent. Unfortunately usually, people take out their frustration on the wrong person for no apparent reason because they have built up stress and are forced to let it out because they know no other way.

The next time someone does this to you, show him or her your unconditional compassionate side by not reacting with equal negativity. Try not to take what the person is doing or saying as personal. Only when we take things personally does it become an inner problem of our own. See it as you are doing him or her a favor. The universe will acknowledge good deeds such as this. The person seeing this kindness from you may even apologize for his or her behavior. It is irrelevant if he or she does or does not. He or she most often will not continue directing that type of energy toward you if you don't show a negative reaction. If you see him or her the next day, treat him or her the exact same way as you would anyone else, and you will be helping the person more than can be said in words. Even if your kindness is not acknowledged from the outside, you can know in your heart that you have done your part.

If you feel someone has done you wrong, try removing yourself from the situation and thinking about how he or she must have felt inside to create such a negative outward force, which seemed to be directed at you. Think about what that person has experienced in his or her life to cause him or her to exhibit such behavior. Replace anger for what he or she did with compassion for who he or she is.

As we grow our consciousness, we become the power outlet in which any negativity sent to us will be soaked up in the form of compassion, forgiveness, and, most importantly, love. When these three feelings of expression become dominant, you can find all power and inner happiness within you because, no matter what negative force is sent to you, you can replace it with a positive feeling to protect yourself and help uplift the world.

Through compassion, we can take a different approach to life, take the negative aspects going on around us less seriously, and sometimes even laugh at them. We can take an entirely new approach to life and begin to witness the world instead of negatively reacting to it. Compassion is another tool we can use to free ourselves from inner negativity. Once compassion for all people arises, we see that we never had to react negatively to the things people have said or done to us because, by having compassion for them, we experience compassion instead of suffering. "If you want to make someone happy, practice compassion. If you want to make yourself happy, practice compassion."(Quote from the Dalai Lama).

Forgiveness

Forgiveness is an automatic consequence of a greater understanding and contextualization of life. When we are thinking in terms of how to best utilize this lifetime for our spiritual growth on the path to find inner freedom and joy, not forgiving is a waste of valuable time and energy. We can put the energy consumed in not forgiving to better use for our internal healing and growth.

The analogy is we have a container (spirit) that is filled with water (energy). The goal is to fill the container (spirit) with as much water (energy) as possible. The more water (energy), the more full (more fulfilled) the container (spirit). Negative outgoing projections and emotions of any kind are like hoses that are attached to the container and drain water (energy) from the container (spirit). Too much outgoing water results in a lack of sufficient water (energy) to maintain the balance of the container (spirit). Positive feelings, intentions, and thoughts can be seen as the tap that fills the container (spirit) with water (uplifting energy). Non-forgiveness drains energy. Forgiveness opens the tap.

Something is only there to forgive when we are holding onto an event that happened in the past. In reality, whatever happened that we are finding it hard to forgive is done already. It already happened. Obviously, the experience was not a pleasant one, or we wouldn't be struggling to let it go. But unfortunately, by not doing so, we force ourselves to experience the unpleasantness over and over. Anger builds up, and we see the person we are unwilling to forgive as the enemy. If we are unwilling to forgive ourselves for something we did, guilt overcomes us. Either way, both anger and guilt are both forms of suffering. For some strange reason, our minds justify holding onto them, and we agree to it. Why?

All suffering is a form of the ego and its limited perception. The ego is a strange little creature that is not about to let something hurtful directed at us go by without a fight. It holds onto negativity with a tight grip. Whatever we are holding onto is now causing equal or more suffering than the actual experience in the first place.

Let's break down why it is hard not to forgive certain experiences. When someone does something terribly wrong to us, we often first think to ourselves how much of a**hole he or she is. Then we go over and over it in our minds: what happened, how it happened, when it happened, why it happened, if it's going to happen again, what we should do next time, what we should have done this time, and so forth. The mind is addicted to going back into a past situation and clinging onto it. Meanwhile, we are just sitting on the couch, watching TV, and eating popcorn while a storm is brewing up inside of us.

Let's think about it on a greater scale. Most people in this world have experienced a situation that was perceived as so terrible that it would almost seem impossible to forgive the person who seemed to cause that inner pain. That person said or did something to us, and it is just too hard to forgive him or her for what happened. The mind says, "I did nothing to deserve what he or she did to me so he or she doesn't deserve my forgiveness." Does this sound familiar? Everyone has to go through this universal experience to different degrees in some point in life. It is like a hurdle we jump over. Some refuse to jump over and crash into the obstacle over and over again. They continue to feel the pain that results from not jumping over it.

The fact is, when we hold onto a grudge or have anger toward someone and refuse to forgive, we feel the suffering of the situation whenever we think about it. Non-forgiveness is a cancer that grows inside of us. And it is only affecting us. The person that did what he or she did has most likely forgotten all about it. He or she may not even have realized he or she did something hurtful depending on the situation. Or he or she might feel really bad and wish he or she could take it back. Whatever he or she feels doesn't affect how you feel. They are two different internal experiences.

In order to make ourselves feel better, we seek to understand what really caused the inner pain in the first place. It has always been a what, not a who. The ego is the only thing on earth that can cause suffering. It does so in two ways: sending out force and internalizing it.

First, the ego sends out force, either physically or verbally, and hides behind the individual. Then, according to the law of force, the force is internalized and released with equal force. Because of this law, problems can never be resolved without the intervention of positive feelings such as compassion, forgiveness, and acceptance.

By resistance to forgive, the ego can feel like the victim and therefore has means and justification for holding onto negative emotions. It is important to remember that we neither like nor want to feel inner adverse energy or feel like the victim. Only the ego inside of us does. The ego hides behind us as us, so we defend its wants as ours instead of pursuing the inner peace we all seek.

We can free ourselves from aspects of the ego by recognizing its fallacies and the addiction it has to defending itself and clinging to the past. We then must take the following position, "The person I really am wants to feel good; therefore, I forgive the ego in myself and others." In doing so, all people are instantly forgiven as just the ego in all of us was the only thing that needed understood and with that understanding comes forgiveness.

It actually feels good to forgive. When we do, we take all the negative built-up energy that was accumulated from holding onto the negative aspects of the situation, and in one instance, we release the negative energy from our auras. Forgiveness is freeing and can be done in an instant.

A Course in Miracles, a self-study curriculum that aims to assist its readers in achieving spiritual transformation, describes a nondualistic philosophy of forgiveness and includes practical lessons and applications for the practice of clemency in one's daily life. If you are looking for an easy course to follow on a daily basis to increase your capacity for forgiveness and compassion, this is a wonderful option.

Humility

Humility means to be humble. To be humble means to not put oneself on a pedestal and look down at situations and others. Humility is to have a modest view of one self. When you surrender seeing yourself above others or life situations, the need to change or control people or situations ceases. The willingness to accept things for the way they are replaces the urge to control to change them.

Actually, the less one is humble, the more tiresome it is. When you see yourself a certain way and build yourself up to something, it puts a sense of pressure on yourself to live up to your own high standards. You have to constantly prove to yourself that you are, in fact, what you have built yourself up to be. This easily leads to negative emotions because, when a situation occurs that is out of your control and forces you to see yourself in a different way, suffering is automatic because, in that moment, you are unable to live up to your own inner expectations. Being humble is the gateway to freedom. It does three very important things:

- It removes the pressure on you to be a certain way and therefore relinquishes a lot of suffering.
- It allows you to seek further knowledge and learn willingly instead of matching new incoming information with your preinstalled belief systems and determining if you can accept the material or not based on if they match your beliefs.

- It removes the need to always be right in every situation and social interaction. A humble person can laugh at his or her mistakes or shortcomings instead of becoming overwhelmed with anger when his or her image of how others perceive him or her is not protected.

Being humble is a good way to live in the world. It allows you to be lighthearted and easygoing and express the true you without always feeling the need to protect and defend yourself. Humility doesn't make someone less important. It makes him or her more likeable. People like humble and innocent people. One can still carry a sense of self-esteem and remain humble. To be humble simply means to drop inner arrogance. Arrogance turns people off anyway. If you want people to like you for who you are, accept yourself completely. People are as comfortable with you as you are accepting of yourself. This statement was made in one of the lectures of Dr. David R. Hawkins, a renowned and highly regarded psychiatrist.

Humility is also the ability to do great things without having to take credit for them. You strive for excellence just for the sake of excellence itself and not for validation. Your satisfaction comes from doing the best you can and being all you can. There is no point in taking sole credit for something anyway when you know the only reason you were able to do it is because you were granted the gift of life and given your inner gifts in the first place.

Gratitude

Gratitude for life is an expression of thankfulness. Being thankful comes from being aware that life did not have to be the way it is or be at all. What if there were no such thing as life with no awareness and no ability to experience anything? What if there were 7 billion humans still but you didn't exist?

Life is all inclusive and includes everyone in the universal experience and that is something to be grateful and happy for. The self sustained happiness can be tuned into at any moment. Life itself is very taken for granted by lots of people, simply because we are looking out through the wrong eyes. Our dominating perspective can sometimes blind us from reality of the miracle of life and all of its expressions. The miracle of living and experiencing in each moment is already perfect and can provide all the happiness one seeks if awakened to the miracle. The problem is we abandon the inner child in us, the one that looked around at everything and was just excited and in awe to experience everything in the moment without thinking of past and future. The inner child that saw everything as if it were seeing it for the first time. The inner child that giggles when they press a button, just because.

Think of it this way...lets say you were born right now, BOOM, you just came into awareness into this world. The first thing you would do is what? Probably be amazed at everything in your new experience and look at everything in awe and excitement. Your pleasure would be obtained from just the experience of life in the very moment.

What can we be thankful for in each moment? We can be thankful for the awareness that we exist. We are blessed with the gift of being alive: looking, feeling, breathing, smelling, hearing, touching, communicating, thinking, and loving. We can be thankful for these miracles, along with thankfulness for our families and friends and everything that people do for each other.

A lot of the time after someone has a heart attack or finds himself or herself in a situation where he or she was close to death, he or she becomes overwhelmed with gratitude for his or her life. Something bad shouldn't have to happen for us to be thankful for it in the first place. The gift of life is the greatest present that could be given.

For example, let's say you were given a box. Inside the box contained everything that is considered to be of great value here on earth, such as billions of dollars, the best cars, keys to mansions, and anything you can imagine you would want. Now let's say the person who gave you the box said you could have all of this, but there is one catch. In order to get everything, you must give up your ability to be aware. So if you choose the box, you will have everything and be able to do anything, but you won't be aware of it. So what would you choose: the box or your awareness?

This simple example illustrates what is really the most precious thing in our lives, our awareness. The ability to be aware of the experience of life exceeds any gift we could ever be given.

The gift of life has already been given. Now it is up to us how we choose to react to the gift of life. Are we thankful for it? Or do we ignore it and continue on the never-ending pursuit to find something else that is better? The choice is ours to make. Embrace and love your life. Enjoy the experience, your on vacation. The vacation called life.

CHAPTER 7

POWER OF LOVE

This chapter explains how to tap into the energy of love and unconditional lovingness. It includes detailed writings on the most powerful, uplifting, and healing energy in the universe.

Introduction to Love

Up until this point, the book has mainly focused on the restricting behaviors, limiting perspectives, and changing one's attitudes and outgoing projections to remove inner suffering at the source in order to reach inner contentment. Now here is where we bring everything together. This is the exciting part. The final most important piece of the puzzle is love.

We are not referring to an emotional love. When the topic is discussed, people relate love as something between two people such as romance and affection. Although this is the common term, the love written about in this book is far different. We use the word "love" just as a word to describe a specific compassionate, uplifting, caring and healing energy. It can be related to as spiritual love or compassionate love. When this specific energy is added to the inner experience, life becomes pleasant, fulfilled and full of joy.

Imagine life as a chocolate cake. The cake by itself is fine, but icing is missing. Love is like the icing on the cake. When it is added, the cake is just so much better. The same goes for life. When love is added to life, the experience is more enjoyable. We know this from experience, but for some reason, we find it hard to smother our cakes in icing. Maybe we feel a little guilty or another dominating emotion is not allowing us to do so. But for whatever reason it is, it can't be more important than having a cake full of delicious icing.

At times, our cakes look like a droopy-eyed gorilla with one arm responsible for the icing department. A big blob in one corner and little dabs are here and there, but the majority of the cake remains uncovered. Just like the majority of people's lives only have a limited amount of love spread to the family and some good friends, it is self-rewarding to grow our love and feel the resulting benefits.

Staying with this icing analogy, have you ever made one of those gingerbread houses with all the candy? Icing is the edible glue that holds everything together on the house. Without it, the house would be in little pieces and wouldn't look well constructed. We can compare love to the icing on the gingerbread house. This ingredient holds everything together as one to create beauty and a foundation to build on. Not only that, when you use icing, you can eat it. When you use love, you can experience it.

Another example we can use to describe love is a hot air balloon. Let's say you were excited to experience riding in a hot air balloon. You and your friends got into the basket and waited for the balloon to start rising in the air. You quickly become disappointed to find out that the balloon wasn't rising and all that was happening was a bunch of people standing in a basket.

Instead of looking around to see that a big green button says "Push to fill with hot air," people start blaming one another for why the balloon isn't rising. Fights break out, and the entire experience is ruined.

The hot air balloon needs hot air to fill it to make it float into the air. Without hot air, it is just a flat balloon. Now compare the balloon to our lives and the hot air to love. As human and spirit beings, love needs to fill us to have the experience we are looking to have in this world. We have spent too much time looking around and seeing the person to blame for not having a positive experience that we haven't come to realize we have the power source inside of us all along. Also, a big green button inside of us says "Push here to release love." It is called the heart.

Healing Energy

One energy in this world has the power to heal all suffering: war, dependencies, addictions, abuse, crime, depression, anxiety, trauma, mental illness, bodily illness, fights, cruelty, and fears. And the list goes on forever. Only one energy will ever exist that contains enough infinite power that can literally wash away a problem with its very presence. This energy is the word we call "love."

The power of love can heal, repair, restore, rejuvenate, elevate, and uplift. With the presence of love through the expression of lovingness, our inner experiences become enjoyable. Not only that, our bodily cells react in a remarkable manner. When one is in the state of lovingness, the body begins to repair damaged cells and replace them with healthy components that heal diseases at astonishing rates of recovery. The energy of love puts our bodies into a miraculous recovery mode that lets the body's defense and repair mechanisms work at fast speeds to bring us back to our normal homeostasis.

Love is transformative. It alters the inner experience of life, the way our bodies sustain themselves, the way people respond to you, and the way life is experienced. If everyone loved, there would be no fights, abuse, cruelty, crime, war, or need for punishment. Love is the answer to all problems we find in the world, both on an inward scale and what is going on externally.

Love Is Everywhere

Love is an inner experience, although it can be expressed externally where it is seen as an act of caring kindness or sacrifice for something else. Numerous life experiences as well as videos touch your heart in a way that words sometimes can't. These acts of love inspire the world in a direct way other than knowledge. Love is everywhere in the world. You just have to be open to see it. Here are some of nature's expressions of love:

- A puppy jumps into a pool and struggles to swim. Another dog dives into the pool to save the puppy and pulls it out to safety.
- A squirrel gets lost from its family. A cat adopts the squirrel and nurtures and loves the animal like it is one of her kittens.
- A dog breaks its leg. The owner takes the dog outside every day, holding up the doggy with a sling and helping him walk again to strengthen the leg again.
- An elderly couple in their nineties, who have been together their entire lives, get excited to go for a walk every morning at seven and hold each other's hand as if they just fell in love.
- A person drops flakes of food into a fish bowl.

- The male penguin keeps the baby penguin's egg warm by standing over it for up to sixty-five days without eating.
- A cat and dog cuddle.
- Someone puts a jacket around a homeless person who is cold.
- A homeless man dives into a freezing lake to save a child from drowning.
- An orangutan and dog become best friends. The orangutan hugs the dog and smiles.
- A lion and baby calf meet in the wild. The lion adopts the baby calf as her child instead of seeing the baby calf as food.
- A women goes through pain to give birth to a human being, and the baby wraps its hand around the mother's finger for the first time.
- A hunter shoots a duck, and it falls to the ground with a broken wing. Another duck comes swooping down and surrounds the wounded bird by covering it with its wings and protecting it from the hunter.

The power of love made all of these possible. Nature is instinctively loving, kind, compassionate, caring, and open to helping others. Lovingness sprouts from an inner choice to align oneself with how nature intended to express itself. The people who are truly making a difference in the world are those who choose love above all else.

Inner Love

The inner effects of loving are uplifting and extremely enjoyable. Most people have felt the experience of inner love in some areas of their lives. Whether it is for their children, family members, the pet, or something in the world, the inner feeling of pure genuine love is experienced the same, no matter what it is exhibited toward.

Inner love is a sense of comfort, extreme pleasantness, fulfillment, sustained satisfaction, enjoyment, pleasure, and an overall joyous inner experience. This is why we want more love in our lives. It feels so good! The point is to get drunk on love so you don't need anything else.

Inner love has no restrictions other than us withholding it back because we feel something else is not worthy of our love. Love has no limitations. It can be consistently on or turned on and off. We make the choice.

Feeling Good

The primary goal of life for the majority of people is to feel good and have a positive life experience. If we are serious about this, we need to make the connection between feeling good and the way to feel good.

It is like we want to go swimming, but we refuse to fill the pool with water. Then we dive into the pool, land on cement, wonder why it hurt, and continue to do the same process over and over again, never making the connection that we need water in the pool to swim. The same goes for our lives. Once we honestly make the connection between what it takes to feel good and how we do it, we can start taking the necessary measures to reach our goals.

Just as the pool needs filled with water in order to have an enjoyable swim, love needs to fill our hearts in order to have an enjoyable life. There is no way around this universal truth. The sooner we make the connection, the quicker we can feel good living.

God's nature is for all to have an amazing life experience. That's the whole point. We have been given everything we need to make that possible. Everyone has the potential to be happy, the ability to be kind and compassionate, and the power to love. Now it is up to us to be responsible beings and use our love the way it was meant to be. Let's be all we can be in this life, maximize our energy potentials, and use the powers we carry in our hearts with excitement and joy.

The Opportunity

It is a blessing to be born a human being. We have the free will and ability to love anytime. With this blessing comes an opportunity. Not only do humans have the ability to experience love, but we can evoke the experience of love and release it under no conditions. With the power of our hearts, we can do this. We can take love from being conditional to unconditional and express it toward all aspects of life. We can take love from being restricted to being released, from being held back in our minds to being radiated out in the form of compassion, forgiveness, and lovingness.

Only the human being was created with the inner capability to reach this state. We are more than blessed to be human beings and have this unique opportunity fix our karma, expand our consciousness, and grow our love.

There is a way to express our gratitudes for the opportunity God has provided us. We express our appreciations through dedication to make the mind parallel with the heart. When we align our minds with our hearts, we experience the uplifting power of our hearts within our minds. The mind becomes a pleasant experience where everything negative is filtered away and love and compassion remain primary.

With this universal opportunity each of us has been granted, we can make it a primary goal in this life to fulfill our potentials through love and respect for ourselves, others, and God. We choose to dedicate our lives to lovingness based on the gratitude that arises through understanding the gift of life and awareness of existence. When we realize, acknowledge, understand, and appreciate the gift of living (life), it gives us a permanent reason to emit our love for the world and fulfill not only our potential but our lives' purposes taking us one step closer to our destinies.

Choosing Love

To choose love as a primary way of being in the world is a powerful decision indeed. It is the ultimate choice of all choices that can bring about good health and carry you joyfully through every single aspect of life because of the pureness of its intention. When one becomes dedicated to this choice and devoted to love above all else, something miraculous takes place, the feeling of being complete arises as a continuous experience, something we have always been looking for.

Devoted does not mean loving in this moment and not in the next. Nothing can happen with this type of half effort. Maintaining inner love has to become more important than anything else to get results. When full effort is applied to lovingness as a way of being, a paradigm shift takes place, and the inner experience becomes delightful. What once was seen to cause suffering can now be witnessed as an opportunity to express oneself to his or her maximum potential of loving expression.

What if the unconditional love that a mother has for her children could be spread to the world? What an amazing domain it would be, safe and filled with compassion and protection. It starts with each individual to make the choice inside of him or her to be loving and kind for the sake of its own reward.

Why is it important to choose love? To be in the presence of love is to be in the company of God. When we love others, we give them a piece of God. Every single time you love another person, you are handing him or her a piece of God and giving him or her more power to grow his or her soul in the process of liberating and uplifting your own being. To choose love is to choose God.

Love Restrictions

Spiritual love wants to shine at each moment, but we prevent it with our love restrictions. So why do we put restrictions on our love? We know, if we exhibit love toward something, we will experience it, and it will feel good inside. So why do we hold our love back from certain people or aspects of life? It doesn't make sense if we think about it in terms of maintaining a pleasurable inner experience. The only person from whom we end up withholding love from is only ourselves. By not loving outwards, we can't experience it.

When we are born, we live solely on love. We can see a newborn child's innocence in his or her eyes. He or she only wants to be loved and love back. As our inner children, we love because no reason tells us not to. That inner child is still in us and wants to burst out with joy, but we have to be willing to let it. The innocent child, once so alive and well in each of us, has been placed in the background for too long. It is begging us to release it from the prison we have held it in.

As we were exposed to the pressures and stressors of the world, it is as if sometimes we move farther and farther from our inner loving children. The love we send out becomes conditional, and we take on the belief system that you only send out love when there is a reason. We begin to put restrictions on our love based on perceptions—if they love me, if it is important enough to love, and so forth—and agree with ourselves to restrict our love to certain aspects and people in our lives. We create "love restrictions" and hold onto them with complete seriousness. Rules become involved in the simple act of loving something. Only when all of our predetermined conditions and expectations are met will we release love and experience its uplifting side effects. Isn't that how it goes?

Love restrictions become so dominant and controlling in our lives that we get to the point where it is almost impossible to experience real love. Most people only experience the inner feeling with family, some very close friends, and maybe a pet and withhold their love from everything and everyone else. People view love as something that is limited, as if there is a limited amount of it to go around so you have to choose wisely where you use it. This isn't true. In fact, it is the opposite.

The more loving you become, the more love you have to give. Nevertheless, because the average human being is so picky and choosy with his or her love, there is a feeling that something is missing in his or her life, and the pursuit to fill the void begins. Material and glamorized lives become the primary goal in life in an effort to fill the missing feeling. The attempt to satisfy the inner experience with external toys and pleasure sources prevails in order to fill the hole created by the lack of love. The pursuit to find happiness and pleasure in the world dominates and replaces the always available inner spiritual love that is waiting to be released at each moment. "Seek the kingdom of heaven within." In other words, seek the love within.

Everything you have been seeking to get in the world is only a black-and-white comparison of what can be obtained internally. Although it may seem like love is obtained externally, it is an internal and ever-present experience when unconditionally awakened. For example, we can see how we actually experience this feeling by just thinking about it. When someone loves you, do you feel what he or she is feeling inside and pick up on it and therefore feel good? No. So how do you feel love? Like everything, you only feel something if it is coming from you. For example, if someone is upset with you while driving home in his or her car, you don't know he or she is upset with you. Just as well, if someone is loving you while driving home, again, you didn't feel anything. In truth, we only experience the full powers of love when we are the one loving.

Many people feel like they have not been loved enough and therefore refuse to give their love to others. It is very sad to see when people feel like no one loves them because then they don't feel like they have a reason to love either and the experience is restricted from their lives. It is true in the sense that some people seem to receive more love than others do as they grew up, but these factors are out of our control. Every person goes through the life experiences that will be best for his or her spiritual growth. No two life experiences can be compared. No matter how much love you have or have not felt up until this point does not change how much inner love you can feel in your life.

People feel lost when they don't see anything worth loving in their lives. Fortunately, most people have some sort of outlet to release love like a pet, life partner, or family member, and this sustains their temporary well-being. Just having a few loving thoughts counteracts thousands of negative thoughts in a day and helps balance the system.

The majority of humanity has the mentality of always looking to get something from people. It is beneficial to stop trying to get something from people that they are unable to give you. Instead, become the giver. Instantly, the thought may arise, "Well, what's in it for me?" When you give, you get what you give. Rather than being frustrated waiting for people to give you love, validation, and respect, give it to them instead. Give people love, validation, and respect. Everyone deserves these gifts.

When told to just love everybody, the usual response is "Yeah … right." Attempting to love everyone is just too overwhelming. The love has to start from somewhere within us and grow. It is like a seed that sprouts and blossoms into a beautiful flower. First, simply love that you have life. Love that you are something. Then move to loving who you are as a person. See yourself as an innocent life-form worthy of love. Then extend that love to nature, maybe animals, because it is easier to see the innocence in them. Take one step at a time. Eventually when you are comfortable with your inner state and feel like you have grown to love yourself and the world, move onto loving other people. See the innocent side of people who are just trying their best, and love that quality in them. Love others as much as you have grown to love yourself. This is the process of removing love restrictions that have been established over years. This doesn't mean you have to go around hugging everyone you see and saying "I love you." It is just an silent inner state of being and relating with life.

When you maintain inner lovingness as a common expression, you are serving God, yourself, every single person on earth and the entire universe. You are literally uplifting the world with the positive energy that radiates from your being and up into the field of consciousness.

When you are in the presence of an unconditionally loving person, you will feel a little better than you do when you are not with him or her. This is because of the energy that is radiating off him or her carries calming and healing properties. If you are talking to him or her—and let's say you are upset—anything you send to him or her in the form of negativity will be soaked up with compassion and released with positive energy. If you are with him or her long enough, the feeling of being upset will automatically begin to subside, and you will feel more at peace because he or she will never send you any forceful energy or put you in a situation that you are uncomfortable. So we yearn to be with loving and caring people.

When is it appropriate to love? Different people will have a variety of answers, but for a person who wants to feel good and sustain it, the answer is that it is always appropriate to love. It doesn't have to be directed toward specifics. It just needs to be exhibited to be experienced.

Expect nothing from loving others. A person can call you ugly tomorrow, and you can still love him or her or maintain your inner lovingness. Who said you can't? If you stay in the field of loving energy, the world will change around you. Love is attracted to love. So when you send it out into the universe, the field of consciousness sends it flying back to you without exception.

Once this inner lovingness arises, all internal suffering will be abandoned and fail to play a factor in your life. The only thing experience that will remain is complete and absolute, unwavering happiness, joy, peace, serenity, and reverence for all life, and it will continue to grow.

Follow Your Passion

A lot of people do not like what they do in life and therefore carry an unsatisfied outlook. Loving is the last thing they think about doing which is understandable. If your not satisfied with what is going on in day to day life, loving is not going to be your go to feeling of expression.

It is beneficial to create a life doing the things we love as it rubs off on all areas of our life. If we feel we are forced to do something we don't want to do, we are susceptible to feel like victims and have reasoning to support our negative emotions.

When people are exposed to an environment they don't want to be in and when they do not love what they do, they carry this unsatisfied outlook into other areas of their lives. For example, Ryan feels he is forced to work as a plumber to sustain a living for his family. He hates his job and never wants to go to work. Every day, he wakes up with a negative attitude, goes to work, and carries that adverse perception with him throughout the day. Ryan has no passion for plumbing, and because he does not enjoy what he is doing, during and after his work shift he feels drained.

He feels trapped and waits for the weekend to come because he will then have some freedom from what he doesn't like to do. The lack of doing what we loves, affects his whole life.

It is beneficial for our own inner happiness to follow our passions and do what we love. If we have passion for something, we automatically do a good job and experience joy when we are doing it; therefore, we will have success doing it. If we love to do something, we look forward to it and bring a positive energy into the situation. If you do what you love and are passionate about, it will change every aspect of your life for the better. Like the saying goes, "If you do what you love, you love what you do."

Sometimes it takes courage and moving beyond one's fears to make a change in life and to follow ones passion. Are you working at your job because of the money or because you love what you do? It is good question to ask oneself. Of course it is not always as easy said than done when trying to maintain survival and good life for our families but it is a good general rule to do what you love and create your life around your passions.

Ryan secretly always wanted to be a chef. He loves to cook, and his passion allows him to look forward to making delicious food and enjoy every moment of it. He decides to quit his plumbing job and become a cook at one of his favorite restaurants. Now he wakes up in the morning, excited to go to work to fulfill his passion. He is happy to do what he loves, and he loves to do the best he can at it. He brings this joy home with him for his entire family. The positive energy spreads to each person, and by doing what he loves to do, Ryan has created a better environment for him and everyone around him. He experiences inner happiness and feels fulfilled doing what he enjoys. He is now free to expand his love for what he does into a greater love for life itself.

Falling in Love with Life

To experience love, love life and the experience of living. The point is to fall in love with life. Forget about trying to love everybody individually in the world. This is too overwhelming at first. Simply love the energy of life and the experience of being.

Can you say to yourself that you love life? Once you can say this with honesty and sustain it, your inner feeling will forever change. When you love life, you love all existence and everyone included because the core and essence of everyone and everything is the energy of life. This is true unconditional love. Love the life in you and everyone else. It is all the same. The energy of life is the energy of love, so what you are really doing in the process of spiritual discovery is aligning yourself with life and love.

The energy of life is all loving. If it weren't, why would it have created you? The energy of life is all forgiving. If it weren't, the moment you did something bad in your life, you would have lost the privilege of living. Life is everything it needs to be for us to grow.

Here is the kicker. You don't have life. You are life! How aware are you that you are life? This determines the level of awareness/ consciousness. The more aware you are that you are the energy of life contained in a physical body, the more empowered and ecstatic you feel. The body is a vehicle that carries the energy of life within. So when people tell you to look within, they mean you are to look to the deeper core of your existence beyond the body and mind. Look to the inner energy that radiates from you, the energy of life and love. This is who you truly are. This is what you were meant to identify with as self.

What am I? I am life. Life is God. God is love. Love is life. Therefore, I am love.

Becoming Love

If the source of our existence is infinite love, we too are on the path to becoming this. We choose to come to earth to grow our inner love. Unconditional love is the destination. To get there requires no restrictions, conditions, or expectations for sending out love energy and to simply do it out of respect for thankfulness to God and ourselves.

People are wondering, "How do I make the world a better place?" By becoming loving, you make the world a better place for yourself and all of humanity. A loving person won't start an argument or cause pain and suffering and will never send hateful energy but rather diffuses it.

A loving individual changes the world by example, and the light that radiates from him or her helps to counteract the negativity in the world. If everyone reached this state of lovingness, there would be no war, crime, cruelty, and human suffering. Everyone could be trusted as one big family. This is the proof it is the ultimate purpose. The state of lovingness brings happiness, harmony, and joy to all.

Consciousness and Love

The purpose of life from a spiritual perspective is for consciousness to find its way back to love. The choice to grow consciousness is available whenever one is ready. We can continue to go through the same roller coaster of experiences because of the mind's relentless hold to restrict love. That is why we see over seven billion people on the earth, spirits who seek to raise their consciousness level to that of love and search for a way to do so in their own time. It is how you have found your way here and why you are interested in reading this book right now. We are all united, learning together and striving to reach our potentials for unconditional love.

Loving thoughts bring consciousness into the field of love. No matter what the time of the day, what we are doing, where we are, who we are with, what's going on in the world, or what someone just said to you, the choice to love is always present. When we make the choice, it realigns our consciousness into the energy field of love and brings about the feeling we are seeking.

This is the secret of all enigmas. It was actually not a mystery at all, but it was so hidden in the minds layers of disguises that it seemed to be unknown. To help us find it, we can always present the following question to ourselves, "What do I want to feel in this very moment?" In the background, our inner spirits yell "Love!" while the mind tries to hide it by giving us all the reasons why we shouldn't love in that very moment.

Again, present yourself the question, "What do I want to feel in this very moment?" And then answer, "Okay, I want to feel love. Hmmm … Maybe I should think some loving thoughts." And God takes care of the rest.

Unconditional Love

Unconditional love means to love without conditions. To reach this state of unconditional lovingness requires the detachment of looking at stuff as good and bad or right and wrong. Over seven billion people in the world are determining in their minds what is right and wrong, reacting to that, and changing their inner feeling based on that reaction. Does there really need to be another? Every soul has the intrinsic potential to be relating with life with unconditional love consistently and not determining their inner feeling from the external world of perception. The external world will always be the way it is. It has been like this forever. We first accept this world for what it is, stop trying to change it and put our focus on our own inner growth and lovingness.

If we hold onto this way of seeing something as either good or bad, there will always be a reason to withhold love if something is perceived as wrong or bad. The instant we do this, we have determined with ourselves that some situations or people are not worth loving. The fact is, if something is perceived as wrong or bad, it probably is in need of loving energy to help heal it. If we refuse to give love to the people or situations that are actually in need of it, how do we expect them to get better and change their ways? It is almost hypocritical because people say they want the world to be a better place, but when it comes down to it, how willing are you to actually be the one that is releasing the energy of love capable of making the world a better place? It is something we should think about. You don't have to love someone or something someone is doing that is considered socially incorrect. You simply maintain your inner lovingness.

For example, you hear someone committed a crime and shot someone, which resulted in a death. You don't love the situation because it is impossible to love that. You simply have deep compassion and maintain your inner love as a primary experience so it can radiate out to help all involved and provide healing and recovery. Let's say beforehand you are happy and love-filled. Then you watch something or are exposed to a situation that is considered bad, and it makes you sad and devoid of love. This means based on your perception of what is taking place, you are allowing something in the external world control your inner domain. If you don't want external factors to control your inner feelings, you maintain what you want to feel in each moment, no matter what. It doesn't mean you are a bad person when something bad happens and you don't react negatively. It is when one understands life to the degree that you realize the importance of maintaining your inner love.

Unconditional love means to be that love. You literally become the love so the choice of loving or not in each moment fades away, as you simply "are it." It is easy to love something that is cute, innocent, and loveable. But the people who are serious about reaching the state of unconditional love maintain their inner lovingness in all situations. It doesn't mean you have to go around smiling everywhere and hugging people. It's an inner state of well-being.

To continue our journeys to unconditional love, we realize that only one thing can hold us back from experiencing love at every moment, a resistance to sending it out. We have been programmed to believe that love is only supposed to be sent out under certain conditions that our minds tell us are appropriate. Understand that this is an illusion. By restricting sending out love in this moment, you are only limiting yourself from experiencing love in this moment.

Unconditional love can become a way of life. You can become the outlet to allow all incoming negative energy to be transformed in positive, healing, uplifting, compassionate, and loving energy.

You will know when you have reached this state by the comforting, at-home, and uplifting feeling that the powerful energy field of love washes over you. Just imagine a time where you felt an explosion of love for something. Now multiply that by ten, add a feeling of joy to the mix, and imagine it was consistently your primary experience. That is unconditional love.

Unconditional love can heal all suffering. Reaching this state is the purpose of our lives. Once we make the decision to dedicate our lives to reaching this state of awareness, negativity becomes secondary, and love becomes primary. Joy eventually becomes overwhelmingly present, and the delightful experience that arises makes the struggles of the journey all worth it.

To love unconditionally and see the true essence and beauty of life, we make a decision to become spiritual aspirants to serve the good of humanity instead of seeing ourselves as separate individuals looking for gain in some way. The following are five reasons why love is worth pursuing as a way of being:

1. Love is free. Anyone—anywhere and anytime—can do it.
2. Love feels amazing. The inner feeling is self-sustained and better than drugs.
3. Love helps others. The energy is healing and uplifting to all.
4. Love is our lives' purpose. It is why we came to earth.
5. Love is our ultimate destiny. Eventually, we will pursue it so there is no use waiting.

Clear your mind, fill your heart, and get drunk on love and high on life.

Love with Joy

As lovingness becomes common and automatic, it expands into an inner joy. No gain is necessary with love and joy. All is complete. The joy that is experienced is an aspect of consciousness becoming excited and thrilled that it is finding its way "home". Nothing we do releases the experience. When the negative qualities in the mind that were editing the perfection of life cease and the choice has been made to be all loving, a new energy can come forth that is naturally joyful. The individual behind the scenes gets to experience the consistent joyous occasion as the movie of life continues. The individual me is not the cause of the uplifting experience but rather an impersonal watcher or experiencer. We can make the analogy that it is like watching a fantastic movie and feeling good when watching it. We don't create the film. All we do is watch life and enjoy it as consciousness takes care of everything.

Don't get frustrated if you feel like you aren't getting anywhere and nothing is happening. Changing the way we relate to the world can take time as numerous unconscious judgments and projections have been established. Just like learning to ride a bike, if we gave up the first time we couldn't do it, we would never get to experience the joy of this activity.

Stay conscious of yourself and what you are projecting to the world. If you maintain unconditional lovingness and devote your life to it, by the power of that pure intention, you will experience love as the commonplace without actually literally doing anything at all. You don't have to consistently say "I love you" in your mind. Love is silent.

The thrill of riding the bike was exciting once we got the hang of it. Now it is easy. It works the same way with how we relate to the world with love. At first, it seems nearly impossible and can seem like a struggle. One can feel frustrated if he or she doesn't feel a change right away. It is important to stick with it no matter what. Devote your life to it. If you live aligned with God's love, its loving grace cannot refuse you.

CHAPTER 8

THE INNER PATH

T he inner path is the route to find self-sustained inner peace. This chapter will elaborate on how to look within yourself to find inner contentment and peace no matter what is happening around you. This is for people who are looking for a deeper understanding of the inward path.

Evolving Consciousness

The inner path is one of evolving consciousness. Just like a video game in which characters advance and evolve throughout, so does the being we carry within us. We evolve from human being to magnificent spiritual being and eventually to the source of life itself. At first, consciousness identifies itself with thought, opinions, forms, and beliefs. As consciousness progresses and evolves, it begins to identify with the underlying energy of life, the energy of love.

What Am I

This life is about finding out what we really are and becoming aligned with the source of life. Right now, we think of ourselves as our individual forms. We identify with what our names are, what we look like, how we act, what we think about, and what everything that goes on in our central experiences.

Spiritual work is about moving beyond form and tapping into the invisible but very present universal life energy that is in all. We stop basing our entire existence on the form self and start to identify with a greater power that is beyond individuality. So, we ask, "What am I?"

When one examines the inner being, he or she sees at the core that he or she is simply a watcher/observer with an underlying silent awareness. We watch our lives from an inner awareness just as if we were watching a movie at a theatre.

Behind the scenes are a set of beliefs. This overall belief system affects every aspect of the experience of the movie that determines our thoughts, reactions, opinions, and emotions. False beliefs give us the impression that we need to change something and they cause suffering as the movie unfolds.

Suffering does not have to exist in our inner experiences. We can experience life in the comfort of well-being. It requires us to modify our belief systems to align with universal truth rather than subjectivity, that is, judgment based on individual personal impressions, feelings, and opinions.

The fact is the core of all beings is silent and unchanging awareness that is universal and the same in all. No one is surviving on anything other than awareness in this moment. When we understand this, we can see everyone is not all that different. What makes us seem different is the degree that people are tuned into this inner awareness and how willing they are to accept it as the source of life.

Awareness allows us to experience life. Without its presence within, you would not have consciousness. And without that, you would not know you exist, and you wouldn't be able to read this book. You have to be aware that you are aware to know you are aware, right? Now, that's a thinker.

Awareness and being able to recognize that we are alive comes out of the divine spirit in us, which connects all of life. So awareness is clearly the source of life. To deny means to say I don't need awareness to know I am alive. It just doesn't make sense. Moving a step further, the source of life is God. God is life, present in all with unconditional love that will forever maintain awareness for everyone.

You are all that is, all that can be, and all that ever will be, the energy of life. Life cannot be extinguished. It lives on forever. That's why it is called life. This is where a spiritual foundation of inner knowingness can sprout and blossom into love and joy. Love your inner life source, and take joy in the everlasting experience of existing.

Silent Awareness

The silent awareness encompasses all. It is the backdrop of our primary experiences. Before anything is possible, awareness has to be present. Because of this, everything else can exist. If there were no sky, there could be no clouds, birds, rain, airplanes, and so on. If there were no water, there could be no fish, boats, and so forth. Just like if there were no silent awareness, there could be no form, thoughts, and experiences.

Stress overloads people, and they crave some sort of peace. The peace we are seeking is found in the silence within us. This is also why teachers always tell us to look within. Within us is a peace that is waiting to be awakened. Right now, it is hidden underneath everything else that is going on in the mind. It is like peace is covered by layers of distractions that can be compared to blankets that need unraveled. Peace is always present, but we have to remove and set aside the blankets and distractions so it can be experienced. In doing so, peace shines forth from the inner knowingness, recognition, and appreciation of being the miracle of life.

So we tap into the silence to find the peace. The silent awareness can be tuned into when we match its frequency. Just like a radio has to be tuned to the right frequency to pick up on the correct station, so does our beings. Instead of listening to the annoying inner talk show we usually tune into that distracts us from peace, we change our primary focus onto the silence that is present before the thoughts. Why?

In the silence awareness, there is no suffering. The silence has no problems, worries or fears. The silence is calm and content. We experience suffering because we tuned into it on the inner radio station. When we turn off the noise and tap into the inner silent presence, inner contentment is automatic. In order to experience the peaceful underlying awareness, we awaken the quiet mind.

The Quiet Mind

The common belief is, "My thoughts are mine; therefore, I am my thoughts." This is not true. It is important to know that you are not your thoughts. They are only a part of you. This plays a significant role in finding freedom from inner suffering.

Thoughts are a mere fraction of the overall experience. This section will focus on how to tap into the quiet mind and reassure it is a positive experience to have a mind without constant babbling thoughts. You won't suddenly become stupid and forget everything. The quiet mind actually makes one smarter and increases the energy capacity to get things done with perfection. The quiet mind is peaceful and comfortable state, and that is why we pursue it.

In everyday life, we usually attach to the thoughts that feel most appropriate to us in each moment. Thinking starts the moment one wakes up and lasts all the way until one is asleep. Throughout the day, how many thoughts are actually constructive? It is an awakening realization that the majority is complete nonsense and has no real purpose. They are basically a form of entertainment that we find hard to shut off. It becomes normal to be drowned in thoughts thinking of the past and the future. Many people like social interaction because it temporarily frees them from their reoccurring thoughts.

Unlocking the quiet mind is surrendering the thoughts of the past and not indulging oneself in the thoughts of the future so the moment can be fully experienced. Constructive thinking in the moment can then be fully utilized when necessary without any other thought distractions. When you are at work, you are expected to think constructively, and this section is not to tell you give up all thoughts, quit your job, and go sit in a corner in silence. What we are explaining is how to tame the mind's addiction to clinging on the past and future so it can become a more pleasurable experience in each moment, no matter what you are doing.

So what is stopping the experience of the quiet mind? People have convinced themselves that thoughts make them feel alive and hold onto their thoughts like a kid protecting its candy or a dog shielding its bone. The first step is making an agreement with yourself that it is okay to let go of constant thinkingness for the reward will be better than the thoughts themselves.

Out of seven billion, very few have experienced even a full hour of mind in silence. This is why, when the subject is discussed, it seems nearly impossible to some that it will actually become an experience. If it has not been experienced, then until it is, it is just seen as a story or something that someone talks about that is quickly fluffed off. For the people who are honestly interested about awakening the quiet mind, they learn about it and then put it into practice so it can become an experience.

It is interesting to know that only 1 percent of the human mind is actively racing with thoughts. The other 99 percent is still, calm, and peaceful (Dr. David R. Hawkins mentioned this in live speech). We are latched onto the 1 percent talking mind because it feels like we depend upon it for our continued existence.

To get freedom from the never-ending thoughts, we tap into the 99 percent of the mind that is silent and full of peace. Thoughts are like the 1 percent of fish in an aquarium, and the 99 percent is the water. The goal is to identify with the water instead of the fish.

Meditation has been used through the ages to tame thoughts and experience the peace of the moment without the ever-talking mind. A variety of methods of meditation has been used over the centuries. Buddhist monks dedicate their lives to meditation. The act of meditation requires complete self-awareness to achieve the desired state of inner peace of mind. One deliberately surrenders attaching to thoughts as they arise in each moment. Those who begin to practice meditation are commonly told to watch their thoughts instead of attaching to them.

One method of meditation is to literally say the word "surrender" and replace the arising thought with the word. Once you say the word "surrender," the thought should disappear. With fixity of focus and complete self-awareness, you can continue to watch thoughts arise and surrender them as they come up. You can do this with open or closed eyes. Some find it easier to start with the eyes closed. At first, thinking may continue to dominant, and it may seem nearly impossible, but with practice and relentless focus, thoughts will begin to slow down, and your mind will become increasingly silent, peaceful, and free from worry. The goal is to have no mental activity at all for the time during your meditation. You accomplish this by becoming one with the moment. Remember, don't try to force your thoughts to stop. Witness them from an impersonal point of view, and don't resist them as they arise. Let them flow through your mind without attachment, and they will slowly fade away. In doing this, you are training yourself into the quiet mind. Results may not be instant, but like anything, practice makes perfect, and continuing to prepare proves to be a very worthwhile venture. People report after doing meditation on a regular basis that they feel calmer and more relaxed throughout the day.

Meditation is used to reach a higher level of awareness for a short period of time. Once you enjoy meditation, you are comfortable with it, and you have practiced surrendering all distracting thoughts, it becomes increasingly easier to get back to this peaceful state when you need some time to relax. Meditation is a great practice to get used to tapping into the quiet mind. When starting, take a half hour or so out of the busy day, and practice meditation maybe in the morning or at night or anytime it feels natural for you.

Don't worry about fear of losing control. Surrendering arising thoughts does not mean you are losing yourself, as a conception isn't even capable of truly being you. For example, if you tell your thoughts to stop, they will not. They might actually increase. If the mind of thoughts were truly you, it would have listened and stopped on your command.

Embrace the quiet mind. It is a good thing. Surrendering thoughts of the past and the future gives you freedom to become your true nature and experience higher states of awareness in the moment of now. Why focus on the mind when we can experience the moment? In other words, why listen to the radio when we get the live show?

The quiet mind is simply a shift in focus. Instead of focusing on thoughts, concentrate your being on the underlying ever-present silent awareness of life. Maintaining your inner attention on the underlying awareness will awaken the quiet, still, and peaceful mind that will unlock a new way of experiencing life.

Connecting to Now

The inner path is about connecting and aligning oneself in the now. The now is:

- all that exists
- the awareness that is cognizant that it is
- the experience of livingness
- the unfading, always present, all-encompassing, and everlasting experience of forever

What creates the illusion that the now is always changing? The mind categorizes in terms of time, an earthly experience that helps us make sense of the world. Time is an illusion in the sense that it fades away when you stop identifying with it.

For example, at any time in our lives, we can pose the following question to ourselves, "What am I experiencing right now?" We notice we are always experiencing the moment of now, no matter when, at what time, or where we pose this question. The moment of now never fades. It is like a light that always shines. As each moment seemingly fades away into the past, it actually remains the very same. Our shift in perception creates the illusion of change. There is only one moment, and it is the moment of now. The reality is that the now is always and forever, and we determine our experiences in it at each instant.

We can also ask ourselves, "What do I want to experience right now in this instant?" When the answer comes to us and we know what we want to feel, we can start identifying with the thoughts that will create the inner experience we desire and surrender unnecessary thoughts. When we know the moment of now is forever, we can start enjoying this moment and make the experience a pleasurable one.

The closer we feel to the actual moment of now, the closer we are to living in reality. Living in the mind creates the illusion of past and future that can bring about suffering. Living in the state of forever creates an inner domain free from suffering and full of silence, peace, stillness, and contentment where we are free to live the life we want to live with no restrictions.

Fixity of Focus

There is a well-known phrase, "Live in the moment." When someone tells you to live in the moment, the response is, "Yes, I know I should live in the moment, but …" There always seems to be a reason why something else is more important than the actual moment of experiencing life in this moment. Why?

The mind/ego automatically fixates on controlling what you feel, want, and need. Without internal awareness on what the mind is doing, we fail to notice it, and the minds never ending entertainment take over our emotions. Surrendering the ego's hold on your feelings requires you to have an internal awareness in which you watch your thoughts with fixity of focus, surrender the nonbeneficial ones, and create your own thoughts to create your own reality.

Fixity of focus means to not waver from doing. Practice fixity of focus on staying connected in the moment of awareness that is experienced in the foreverness of now. Witness how a simple realignment can change your experience of life.

Feeling of Forever

Say to yourself, "I am the freedom of forever." Life is awareness. Awareness is to be conscious, to know you exist. To exist is to have life. If you exist now, you can't not exist later because existence is forever. It is either existence or not. Which one can be proven? We can prove existence because we are alive and aware in this moment. Nonexistence cannot be proven. Existence is life, and it is now. To exist is to be forever. If you are now, you are forever.

If you say you are aware of life but then say you believe in death, then you have not yet realized what life really means and the ultimate nature of your existence. Life itself is forever. You are life; therefore, you are forever.

The feeling of foreverness is within you. When you identify with this feeling of forever and realign your being with the underlying energy of life that cannot be extinguished, you are rooted in reality and grace is free to shine. Say this affirmation even if it doesn't make complete sense yet. "I am the freedom of forever."

Loving Witness

We witness the world as it unfolds before our eyes. It is almost like watching a movie. The movie is always playing, and while we watch, it is engrained into us that we have to react and respond in order to be a part of it. In order to live freely, we become loving witnesses of the movie, not critics or victims. The awareness and realization that the movie is always present but has no effect on how we feel inside is the secret to inner freedom.

At every moment, you can ask yourself, "Am I witnessing the movie? Or am I reacting to it?" If you are reacting to the movie, surrender it, and carry on witnessing and loving the movie of life. Find courage to laugh instead of cry, be happy instead of sad, and excited instead of disappointed. Live your life like it is perfect without that mind constantly telling us otherwise, "Life is and will always be perfect."

Pathway to Freedom

The pathway to freedom is the route we take to become free from the ego, which means freedom from suffering. The path requires the strength and power of the inner spiritual will to guide the way to peace.

Walk the path of freedom with a positive attitude and excitement that you are breaking beyond previous limitations that have stopped you from pursuing your dreams and creating the life you want to experience. Find courage to step out of your comfort zone and break through the walls that stand between you and the inner freedom you are seeking. Take responsibility for your progress. When life gets you down, get back up with an even stronger determination and motivation for inner success. Inspire yourself to reach new heights and allow yourself the love and respect you deserve.

Freedom is like blowing up a balloon. At first, it requires great efforts and may seem tiresome. Air might leak out once in a while in the process, but as you are devoted to continue to blow up the balloon, it becomes easier and less effortless until the knot is tied and the object floats on its own without any continued effort or external help.

You could also see your inner being as a water flotation device. If it is not blown up with air (love), it sinks and goes underwater (suffering). So if you want it to float, it requires some action and effort to fill it with air. It may seem to take some time and feel tiresome to fill the water floatation device with air, but you do it because you know it will be worth it. Once there is enough air pumped in and it is sealed, the water flotation device becomes its full potential, reaching its maximal expression. It floats effortlessly on the water and can even be of service to others and hold them afloat. It has its own inner power to carry the weight without sinking underwater. So if you fill your inner being with love, it will float to freedom with self-sustained power.

Take comfort in knowing you are on your ultimate soul's path and life is supporting you 110 percent along the way. If you follow your heart, nothing can stop you. You are the energy of life, the most powerful thing in the universe, on a mission and here for a purpose.

CHAPTER 9

FINAL INSPIRATION

C losing notes to the book with the final chapter focus on awakening the higher self with inspirational text to live your life with purpose and passion.

The Higher Self

The higher self is the universal "I" that recognizes that I am. The higher self is the infinite consciousness that is conscious of being conscious. The supreme awareness is aware that it is. The higher self is the pure experience of experiencing. It is substrate of existence that knows it exists. The isness knows it is; the beingness is the joy of being. The higher self is the divine potential of consciousness expressed as the ultimate reality. It is the core of life, the aliveness of being alive, and the all knowingness that knows it is. The higher self is limitless, boundless, unlimited, unimpeded, and without end. It is forever or eternal. The higher self is beyond thoughts, beliefs, attitudes, opinions, time, location, sensations, form, and labels. It just is always perfectly perfect. The higher self is blissful in its nature, peaceful in its expression, and unconditionally loving and joyful at its core essence. The higher self is the divine quality that is devoted to being one with divinity. It is the oneness of creation within all life. The higher self is the source of existence as manifest and un-manifest that can only be described as "I am." The higher self is pure love, joy, peace, and bliss.

Retiring the Ego

The ego prevents the experience of the higher self. All forms of suffering come from the ego. The ego is impersonal and present in all human beings to different degrees (except for the few enlightened beings who transcended the ego). There are over seven billion humans all with the same version of the ego running inside of them. It is like a computer program with a certain set of commands and characteristics that overrides the hard drive. Imagine the ego as a CD that was inserted into the computer in order to make the computer function and survive, the computer being the human being. One, the CD was inserted into the computer. The ego's operating system instantly wanted to own the computer, control it, run it, perform its own commands, take it to programs that it wants to run, and claim itself as the sole technology that governs the computer. The computer listens to its commands because the operating system tells it what to do, and the computer sees no other way. The ego's system brings the computer to bad areas of the web (negative emotions) and puts the computer in harm's way for receiving bugs and viruses (suffering and illness).

But what is the underlying fact that the computer is ignoring? The computer doesn't actually have to listen to the ego's operating system. It just was because it didn't see any other way. The computer itself is actually the powerful technology that controls the entire system, and the ego's program is just a function that offers tips on how to use the computer. The computer eventually realizes the functions of the ego's operating system are faulty and not letting the computer itself reach its ultimate potential. The computer (human) decides it wants a fresh new operating system (spirit), one more aligned with what it really wants and not just programmed to do what the ego is coded to do. With this new operating system, amazing programs make the ego's operating system look like a children's toy game. The spirit operating system has programs that are fulfilling for the computer, and it stays clear of bad areas of the web that will harm the machine. Instead, it makes the computer faster, more capable, and better functioning and gives the computer a better online experience filled with fun and enjoyment.

It is time to retire the old ego program and replace it with something new and exciting. The ego has had its time for fun and games. Now it is time for us to be the sole controller of our feelings and life experiences. We need to embrace the greatest technology in the world, the human being, and maximize its potential for well-being. Kindly say to your ego, "I appreciate you maintaining my survival up until this point, but I will take it from here. Thanks!" So the ego's operating system is retired into the background, and the spirit's operating system is installed into the computer. Finally, the spirit's operating system dominates and brings the computer back to homeostasis.

Rise above Fear

Fear holds us back. It says, "No! I can't! Something bad will happen!" Now, it is time to say, "Yes! I can! Something good will happen!" Fear is sprouted when the imagination focuses on something that it doesn't want to happen and fixates on it to the extent it causes anxiety. To break free from fear, we use our imaginations the way they were intended to be used, and rather than focusing on what we don't want to happen, we put our energies into imagining what we do want to happen.

Fear is like a little string tied to our backs that holds us back from doing what we want, becoming what we want to become, pursuing our dreams, and rising to the ultimate potential that we know we can reach. Cut the string. It is of no benefit.

Fear is a force that pretends it has power. Fear has no power except for what we give it. To rise above fear, look it straight in the eyes and say, "Bring it!" Love what you fear. Fear is scared of love; fear has a fear of love. Love has no fear. Overpower your worries with love, and watch them run and hide in the darkness where they belong.

Fear subsides joy. That's why it doesn't belong with us. It prevents us from being the joyful being waiting to burst out inside of us. For a moment, imagine your life with no fear. What would you do differently? How would you feel?

Now whatever came to your mind that you would do differently without any fear was good, right? You would feel good, right? Being fearless is rooted in reality. A life with no fear is based in reality. It is freeing, liberating, enjoyable, and exciting. Fearlessness opens the world to what it really is.

Every time you have a fearful thought, laugh at it. Literally laugh out loud. Its worthy of a laugh. Fear is goofy. It pretends it is big and mighty when it is small and powerless. By laughing every time your mind is thinking fearful thoughts that would provoke anxiety, you are training your subconscious into replacing fear with joy.

As weird as it sounds, when a fear is arising, embrace it. If you resist anything, you are forced to experience it. Let the fear flow out of your consciousness as fast as it arose. Watch the change when there is no resistance. Resistance is like a hand that grabs the fear and says, "Okay, I am willing to listen to you." Take your hands, open your palms, and let go of all fear. It will be okay. No fear is valid unless your survival is in danger. All other fear is an illusion, a lie, a trick, and a deception of the mind. No fear is worth holding onto.

Rise above fear to unlock your concealed potential. Move beyond the wall of fear. Don't just jump up and down on the trampoline getting a glimpse of freedom. Get a ladder, climb up it, and, once and for all, jump over the wall to freedom. Life on the other side of the wall has great possibilities and experiences waiting for you. You are never alone. You have unseen support every step you take, and because of this, you can do anything. Believe in yourself, and live life like you have nothing to lose.

Live in Reality

If you want to feel really good in your inner life experience, it requires the devotion to exist in reality. Reality is that which is based in truth. Living in reality means existing in alignment with life and the way it was meant to be expressed and experienced. It requires the relinquishment of that which is considered falsehood. Falsehood is something that is based on falsity, a lie, illusion, or deception. That which is false doesn't bring long-term peace, love, or joy. For example, fear is false because it is based on an illusion. That is how you know if truth and reality or falsehood and deception back something. If its long term will bring self-sustained peace, love, and joy, it is aligned with truth. If something brings short-term happiness but you have guilt or grief after you do it, it is more than likely not based in truth.

Living your life in reality means you have come to respect your life so much that you will not stand for any suffering to be experienced inside of you. Living in reality is how you give back to life to show how thankful you are for the energy of life/awareness of life and what it has allowed of you. As you live your life in reality and maintain your devotion to the supreme energy of life, you will see positive changes take place in your life. Grace will begin to flow into your being. Love will become more present as a primary experience, and inner joy will follow. Inner contentment and peace will be an automatic unfolding brought on by the new understanding of life, what you are, and the peace of knowing everything will be okay. There is nothing to worry about or fear, and the energy of life takes care of all forever.

Growing Your Light

A spirit is a light body or being of light. The light that shines forth from the spirit accounts for the presence of love. The more love present, the more light will shine from the spirit. It is not visible to the human eye. The relationship to the physical world is the aura, a field of subtle, luminous radiation surrounding a person. Some people claim they can see the aura surrounding people although it is very uncommon.

The light is love. People who have had near-death experiences and went to heaven claim a great being of light greeted them.

> I saw a pinpoint of light in the distance. The black mass around me began to take on more of a shape of a tunnel, and I felt myself traveling through it at an even greater speed, rushing toward the light. I was instinctively attracted to it, although again, I felt others might not be. As I approached it, I noticed the figure of a man standing in it, with the light radiating all around him. As I got closer, the light became brilliant- brilliant beyond any description, far more brilliant than the sun-and I knew

that no earthly eyes in their natural state could look upon this light without being destroyed. Only spiritual eyes could endure it- and appreciate it. As I drew closer I began to stand upright. I saw that the light immediately around him was golden, as if his whole body had a golden halo around it, and I could see that the golden halo burst out from around him and spread into a brilliant magnificent whiteness that extended out for some distance. I felt his light blending into mine, literally, and I felt my light being drawn to his. It was as if there were two lamps in a room, both shining, their light merging together. It's hard to tell where one light ends and the other begins; they just become one light. Although his light was much brighter than my own, I was aware that my light, too, illuminated us. And as our lights merged, I felt as if I had stepped into his countenance, and I felt an utter explosion of love. (Betty J. Eadie *Embraced by the* Light, 40–41)

So if light is love, we are here on earth to grow our inner lights, to become the light of love by making inner love unconditional and ever present. When we leave earth, we carry our lights of love into the afterlife. This is why love is so important. It is not just about loving your family, a life partner, and a few friends. Love is what we become. The love we exhibit and maintain in our lives will shine from our soul and be experienced for eternity. We have the power to shine brighter and brighter. It is like if you really liked chocolate and you worked at a chocolate factory and had all the ingredients to make more and more chocolate. Would you do it? Of course! Right now, we have all the ingredients to create more and more love for ourselves, but will we do it? We should! It is the reason why we are here. We know the great potential this life gives us to fill our spirits with love. It is now solely up to us to make the choice if it is worth shining our lights or restricting it with the shadows of negativity. Life is the mirror. We are the flashlight. The more light we shine into the mirror, the more it reflects back at us.

Without the presence of light, there is darkness. Just like there is darkness without the sun. Without the presence of love, there is sadness and despair. If you want to bypass the never-ending roads of suffering and fulfill your ultimate purpose in life, simply love the light of life. With the light, there is everything we ever wanted—the experience of life, the moment of awareness, and the feeling of love and joy. Once you love the light of your life, you are free.

It sometimes seems like we are all separate lights shining from our own sources, walking on our own paths, but as our awareness rises, it becomes clear that we are actually rays of light shining from the same source. In divine time, we will be reunited with the source's all-encompassing light of love.

Ten Steps to Peace

The following are the ten steps to inner peace and well-being. When you walk the ten steps to peace, you will awaken the inner love cocoon, which is safe, complete, all encompassing, and an all-around pleasant inner experience. Used the term "cocoon" because as one reaches certain states of consciousness there is a sense of a surrounding bubble of love protecting and eminating from your being.

You can live by the following ten statements to create your inner love cocoon. Once you do, the security of inner love and peace will rise above all else. All suffering will subside.

1. Take responsibility for your thoughts and inner intention.
2. Remove all inner judgment for oneself and others.

3. Accept that no one is perfect and everyone is evolving and learning.
4. Separate yourself from the ego and its wants and desires.
5. Witness and observe life instead of dictating and commentating.
6. Accept God as the source of your awareness, and tune into it.
7. Live fearlessly with passion and purpose.
8. Realign with the miracle of your existence.
9. Take joy in being alive.
10. Love the energy of life in all and become one with that love.

Time of Great Change

We are now living in the era of *Homo spiritus* and the age of the Aquarius, where the ego's desires for gain become secondary to the humane needs of the spirit. The spirit's inner need for love, harmony, and unity is now primary.

People, countries, religions, and races will slowly come together and find unity. We are here for a greater purpose that duality has long shadowed. Life will no longer be solely dedicated to individuality and the pursuit of external success. Life is a journey within to find the source of existence, what we are, and how to become one with the divine qualities that each of us carry within.

A deep and profound awakening in our overall consciousness happens as people continue to realize the importance of love and human emotion and the effect they have on the world. This is causing a shift in how people experience and relate with the world. To be living in this time is a great blessing, for now more than ever, one can experience rapid inner growth and spiritual freedom. Our lives will continue to change for the better.

Your Time to Shine

Now this is your time. Create your life with joy.

- Be the author of your life; write your own rules.
- Be the artist; mold your own experience.
- Be the painter; draw your perfect picture.
- Be the engineer; build your own reality.

Live like you're on a mission. Think big, and follow your dreams. Make this life everything you want it to be and more. Realize your unlimited potential, and create success. Make choices that take you closer to your dreams. Every day, there are opportunities. Be open to them. Make peace with enemies. Love them, love yourself and love life.

Believe in something great, and pursue with passion. You can do it. Spread your wings and fly with joy. Don't be afraid to fall. Live fearlessly. Be always joyful because you deserve it. Find purpose. Go with the flow, and take chances. Enjoy all life's blessings. Discover your hidden abilities. Don't be afraid of change. Dive into it. Believe in yourself. Set goals. Take action. Overcome obstacles. Break through them. Turn the impossible into the possible. Be extraordinary. Listen to your heart. Let it guide you. Follow your intuition, and win your life!

Closing Notes

The book provided detailed explanations to that which is actually very simple. Everyone is looking for the common experiences of happiness, joy, inner peace, and love. What are you willing to do to awaken these inner experiences? Are you willing to be happy to experience happiness? Are you willing to be joyful to experience joy? Are you willing to be loving, to experience love? Now ask yourself these final questions:

- Do I appreciate my life?
- Do I realize my life is a miracle?
- Do I love existing?
- Do I take joy in being alive?

These questions determine everything. If any of these questions has a "no" or "sometimes" answer, it is time to turn all the answers into an experiential self-sustained everlasting "Yeah!" And that is all that needs to be done.

Life is great. Every day is a celebration. Every moment is a miracle. Every second is an opportunity. I wish you all the best and hope this book has helped you on your life journey. May love be with you now and forever. Amen.

About the Author

B rayden Hall was born and raised in Winnipeg, Canada. You can find Brayden at his website, www.knowledgeforthesoul.com

Printed in the United States
By Bookmasters